JESUS AND THE OLIVE TREE:
RE-ENGAGING THE MYSTERY

Steven A. Neptune

HarvestNet Publishing

Jesus and the Olive Tree: Re-engaging the Mystery

Published by HarvestNet Publishing
PO Box 6071, Cleveland, OH 44101

ISBN 978-0-578-52501-3

First Edition: June, 2019

Printed in the United States of America

DEDICATION

This book is dedicated to my dear wife, Sylvia Neptune,
whose love for the people, land, and God of Israel is contagious.

CONTENTS

INTRODUCTION

WHAT THIS BOOK IS ABOUT

This book sets forth the proposition that the person Jesus of Nazareth is intimately and inextricably related to the calling of God on the Jewish people—past, present, and future. Given the way history unfolded for the synagogue and the church, this proposal may seem to most as "dead on arrival."

However, several factors in varying degrees have led an increasing number of scholars to rethink some traditional assumptions about what the documents comprising what has come to be called the New Testament teach—particularly with regard to the Jewish people and their future. Some of these include:

- The reappraisal of church teachings regarding the Jewish people in the wake of the Holocaust
- The formation of the modern State of Israel
- The discovery of the Dead Sea Scrolls and their subsequent gradual translations
- The explosion of archeological research
- The rise of "Messianic Judaism"[1]
- The intensified research on historical theological writings regarding Israel

More specifically, Rabbinic Jewish, Messianic Jewish, Roman Catholic,

---

1 For a brief overview of the movement see: One for Israel, "Messianic Judaism and Messianic Jews," https://www.oneforisrael.org/bible-based-teaching-from-israel/messianic-judaism-messianic-jews/?gclid=EAIaIQobChMIlOKju7K43wIVRluGCh3PzwumEAAYASAAEgIp8vD_BwE (accessed July 7, 2018).

and evangelical[2] scholars have been carefully sifting through the myriad of new archeological discoveries and recently translated portions of the Dead Sea Scrolls[3] to give us a clearer picture of second temple Judaism at the time of Jesus. What has emerged from this "Third Quest for the Historical Jesus"[4] is a picture of a very Jewish Jesus whose first followers were all Jewish and whose Gospels and letters testify to, not the replacement of the Jewish people and their aspirations, but the beginning of their realization. Indeed, a 2008 article in *Time* magazine listed "Re-Judaizing Jesus" as one of "Ten Ideas That Changed the World."[5] On a parallel track of research, scholars have also begun to discover or high-

---

2 "Historian David Bebbington also provides a helpful summary of evangelical distinctives, identifying four primary characteristics of evangelicalism: (1) Conversionism: the belief that lives need to be transformed through a "born-again" experience and a life-long process of following Jesus (2) Activism: the expression and demonstration of the gospel in missionary and social reform efforts (3) Biblicism: a high regard for and obedience to the Bible as the ultimate authority, and (4) Crucicentrism: a stress on the sacrifice of Jesus Christ on the cross as making possible the redemption of humanity." – from the National Association of Evangelicals' website https://www.nae.net/what-is-an-evangelical/ (accessed Dec. 04, 2018).

3 In the March/April 2015 issue of Biblical Archeology Review, James C. VanderKam, the John A. O'Brien Professor of Hebrew Scriptures in the theology department at the University of Notre Dame, explains the importance of the Dead Sea Scrolls: "The earliest followers of Jesus and the literature they produced were thoroughly Jewish in nature. As a result, the more one knows about Judaism during the time of Christian origins, the stronger basis we have for understanding the New Testament. And the scrolls are the most significant body of Hebrew/Aramaic literature related to a Jewish group or groups from roughly this time and thus are potentially invaluable for shedding light on the meaning of New Testament texts." – Megan Sauter, "What Do the Dead Sea Scrolls Say About Jesus," Biblical Archeology Society, Jan. 10, 2018, https://www.biblicalarchaeology.org/daily/biblical-artifacts/dead-sea-scrolls/the-dead-sea-scrolls-and-the-new-testament/?mqsc=E3934388&utm_source=WhatCountsEmail&utm_medium=BHDDa ily%20Newsletter&utm_campaign=ZE8A2EZ50 (accessed Feb. 5, 2018).

4 David Mishkin, "Introduction," in *A Handbook on the Jewish Roots of the Christian Faith*, ed. Craig A. Evans and David Mishkin (Peabody, MA: Hendrickson Publishers, 2019), 1–3. See also Ben Witherington, III, *The Jewish Quest: The Third Search for the Jew of Nazareth* (Downers Grove, IL: IVP Academic, 1997).

5 David Van Biema, "Re-Judaizing Jesus," *Time* magazine, vol. 171, no. 12, March 24, 2008, 17. To cite only one example of this phenomenon, Amy-Jill Levine, a professor of NT at Vanderbilt University, has teamed up with Marc Z. Brettler of Brandeis University and 34 other Jewish scholars to produce the *The Jewish Annotated NT* (Oxford University Press). Levine, who teaches students preparing for Christian ministry at Vanderbilt Divinity School, hopes *The Jewish Annotated NT* will help Christians understand the Jewish context of their faith and help Jews see that the Christian Scriptures are not only informative about Jewish history, but are also in many places "beautiful and profound."

light the writings of theologians throughout the centuries who also affirmed the continuing significance of the Jewish people as a group in the plan of God as well as their future restoration.

WHY THIS BOOK WAS WRITTEN

While I have been enthralled to read these scholarly works, I have grown increasingly frustrated that I have not found a sort of "one-stop-shopping" book that gathers the distilled essence of all of these rich insights into one short, accessible volume. This book is an attempt to fill that void by taking the findings of the scholars and making them available, in sort of a CliffsNotes[6] form, for the benefit of the general reading public.

COMING TO TERMS WITH TERMS

Obviously, the only way we can meaningfully talk about Jesus and his relationship to the Jewish people is by reference to the Bible, the Scriptures. Now traditionally, Christians have related the "Big Story" of the Bible as one of old and new—enshrined in the practice of designating the Scriptures written prior to Jesus's coming as the Old Testament and those generated after his coming as the New Testament. However, the "New Testament" itself simply refers to both writings as "the Scriptures."[7] I ascribe nothing nefarious to this *old/new* convention. The word *old* carries for us positive denotations and connotations of *that which has gone before*, perhaps *prior* and therefore having *priority* or *first*, *ven-*

---

6 CliffsNotes are a series of student study guides available primarily in the United States. The guides present and explain literary and other works in pamphlet form or online.

7 Examples include but are certainly not limited to—Paul, speaking of the corpus of the "Old Testament" and declaring, "All Scripture is breathed out by God and profitable for teaching, for reproof, for correction, and for training in righteousness" (2 Tim. 3:16); and Peter equating Paul's writings with the "Old Testament": "And count the patience of our Lord as salvation, just as our beloved brother Paul also wrote to you according to the wisdom given him, as he does in all his letters when he speaks in them of these matters. There are some things in them that are hard to understand, which the ignorant and unstable twist to their own destruction, as they do the other Scriptures" (2 Pet. 3:15–16).

erable and therefore *to be honored*, *tried and true* and therefore *foundational.* But *old* can also populate our minds with negative concepts of that which is *outdated*, *worn out*, *obsolete*, and perhaps even that which is the potential *enemy* of the *new*, the *better*. After all, who wouldn't desire the latest iteration of the *new* technology, the 10.0, versus the *old*, *limited*, and now *obsolete* 7.3 for which no tech support is offered? Who wouldn't want to use the *new* and *improved* detergent that will get your linens much whiter than the *old* stuff?

This little linguistic excursus might seem overly pedantic to place at the beginning of the introduction to a book: "Just get on with it, man—tell 'em what you're gonna tell 'em, tell 'em, then tell 'em what you told 'em—that's the success formula for any writing, whether a letter or a book." But I *am* telling you what I am going to tell you. Ideas have consequences. Ideas are encapsulated in words. Therefore, words matter, e.g., "And God said . . . " (Gen. 1:3); "In the beginning was the Word . . . " (John 1:1)! A central theme of this book is about the necessity of getting the "Big Story" of the Bible "right"[8] and how in some very important respects, both Jewish and Christian traditional readings have gotten it wrong. And the mental furniture of "Old" and "New" Testaments[9] has *seminally* contributed to the problem. So at the very beginning of our explorations of how to think "more biblically" about the

8 The following observations attenuate our noble goal in doctrinal matters of "getting it right": "Although truth is a unity and is absolute, our human understanding and doctrinal expression of truth are always partial, incomplete, and less than comprehensive." – Robert M. Bowman, Jr., special projects editor for the Christian Research Institute; "All theological formulations are, at best, approximate." – Walter Elwell, editor of the *Evangelical Dictionary of Theology;* "we recognize that there is no aspect of our lives that is unaffected by our estrangement from God. Even our best endeavors and highest aspirations are prone to sin and error. Forms of faith and life in the church are no exception. This is why Reformed confessions tend to have their own built-in disclaimers. The preface to the *Scots Confession* invites all readers to offer correction from Scripture if they find the confession to be in error." – Anna Case-Winters, Presbyterian theologian. These citations and references can be found in my book *The Promise of the Spirit: Why Now?* (Cleveland, OH: HarvestNet Publishing, 2017), 119–120, and are used by permission.

9 Of course, the "Old Testament" itself announces the coming of a new covenant and its implications and relation to the first or Mosaic covenant are explored in the "New Testament." But it is a serious category error to equate the entire corpus of the "Old Testament" with the contents of the Mosaic covenant.

grand narrative of the Scriptures, we would do well to acknowledge the potential pitfalls associated with designating the Scriptures in the traditional way. There has got to be a coming to terms with *terms!*

Now it would be nice if we could all just refer to the whole Bible as "the Scriptures" and call it a day. But there is no question, from a Christian perspective that is, that with the coming of Jesus there came further revelation, i.e., Scripture, and it seems that it is not only helpful but indispensable to be able to refence this reality with a distinguishing term. So in this work I will be using *Tanakh,*[10] the term traditionally used by the Jewish people, to refer to the "Old Testament" portion of the Scriptures. It is merely descriptive of its contents and does not carry any connotative, negative baggage.

How to designate that portion of the Scriptures which has traditionally been referred to as the New Testament is a bit more tricky. For example, there is currently no settled alternative utilized within Christian/Jewish dialogue circles. To refer to them as the "Greek Scriptures" seems to ignore the *Septuagint.*[11] To use "Apostolic Writings" carries the double weakness of having no convention behind it as well as the connotative pitfall that it could imply something less than divinely revealed,

---

10 "Tanakh, an acronym derived from the names of the three divisions of the Hebrew Bible: **T**orah (Instruction, or Law, also called the Pentateuch), **N**evi'im (Prophets), and **K**etuvim (Writings)." Encyclopaedia Britannica, "Tanakh," https://www.britannica.com/topic/Tanakh (accessed Dec. 04, 2018). Notice how Jesus refers to the Scriptures in Luke 24:44–45: "Then he said to them, 'These are my words that I spoke to you while I was still with you, that everything written about me in the Law of Moses and the Prophets and the Psalms must be fulfilled.' Then he opened their minds to understand the Scriptures."

11 "*The Septuagint* (from the Latin: *septuāgintā* literally "seventy," often abbreviated as LXX and sometimes called the Greek Old Testament) is the earliest extant Greek translation of the Hebrew scriptures from the original Hebrew. It is estimated that the first five books of the Old Testament, known as the Torah or Pentateuch, were translated in the mid-3rd century BCE and the remaining texts were translated in the 2nd century BCE. Considered the primary Greek translation of the Old Testament, it is quoted a number of times in the New Testament, particularly in the Pauline epistles, by the Apostolic Fathers, and later by the Greek Church Fathers." Wikipedia, "Septuagint," https://en.wikipedia.org/wiki/Septuagint (accessed Jan. 3, 2018). I understand that in academic circles it is considered inappropriate to use *Wikipedia* as a reference. But I take the view of Dr. Jordan Peterson who writes "I cite Wikipedia because it is collectively written and edited and, therefore, the perfect place to find accepted wisdom." Jordan B. Peterson, *12 Rules For Life: An Antidote to Chaos* (Toronto, Canada: Random House Canada, 2018), 114.

authoritative Scripture—on a par with the Tanakh. So it would seem prudent for the present moment that I stick with the conventional "New Testament," hereafter designated NT.

As you proceed through the book, you will discover that there are other key terms, e.g., *Israel*, *Church*, and *New Earth*, that we need to come to terms with if we are to have any hope of getting the Big Story of the Bible right. Like the discussion above concerning how to think about the Scriptures, each of these terms has a long, interpretive history behind it that affects how we view God's grand plan for his creation as revealed to us in his word.

The Structure

The book is divided into nine chapters. I am aware that not only the central proposition of this book invites a measure of initial skepticism, but each chapter contains elements that are open to challenge. While I cite scholars to support that which is being asserted, the primary tenor of this little book is declarative, not apologetic. I would invite the reader to pursue the sources cited in the footnotes for a fuller defense of each step of the argument.

In chapter one, "Re-engaging the Mystery," I point out that there is subject matter in the Bible, designated as *mystery,* which the church has wrestled with over the centuries—often accompanied by great controversy—before a settled, universally agreed upon articulation emerged. But there is one mystery, the mystery of Israel and its relationship to Jesus, which has not received this kind of attention. In fact, only *one*, rather simplistic view of this mystery—*Supersessionism* or *Replacement Theology*[12]—emerged early in the history of the church. It remained the unchallenged reigning orthodoxy for 17 centuries until a radical alternative

12 *Supersessionism/Replacement Theology:* God used the Jewish people to bring forth the Messiah, but once he has come, "ethnic" Israel has served its purpose and is no longer relevant to the plan of God, except to serve as an exemplar and warning to others of the consequences of unbelief. The church, primarily Gentile in nature, has *superseded* or *replaced* the Jewish people as the people of God and is now the "true Israel."

called *Dispensationalism*[13] arose circa 1830 to challenge it—at least in some evangelical circles. This state of affairs begs for a re-engagement with this mystery which is now happening in our generation.

In chapter two, "Development or Deviation," I point out that scholars of church history recognize and lament the relative paucity of information we have regarding developments in the church in the time between the apostle Paul's death under Nero in the mid-sixties and the beginning of the second century. This is because the picture of the church as portrayed by the Apostolic Fathers[14] seems quite different from that which is portrayed in the NT. This reality invites the question as to whether these changes are for good, or bad—are they signs of unfolding and development, or diversion and deviation? My very informal and partial survey of church historians would seem to suggest that the majority take a *both/and* approach. In the case of Israel, it strikes me and many others that *deviation* is the unrelenting rule.

In chapter three, "Jettisoning the Jewish Connection," I start with the writings of the early second century Gentile leaders of the church and trace their step by step disassociation with all things Jewish through to Augustine in the early fifth century. Here we witness the germination of the seeds of Supersessionism into the full-flowered Replacement Theology which reigns unchallenged by a *systematic* response for seventeen centuries.

In chapter four, "Dispensing with Dispensationalism," I start with

---

13 "*Dispensationalism* is a religious interpretive system and metanarrative for the Bible. It considers Biblical history as divided by God into dispensations, defined periods or ages to which God has allotted distinctive administrative principles. According to dispensationalist theology, each age of God's plan is thus administered [*dispensed*] in a certain way, and humanity is held responsible as a steward during that time." Wikipedia, "Dispensationalism," https://en.wikipedia.org/wiki/Dispensationalism (accessed Oct. 1, 2017).

14 Apostolic Fathers is a term coined in the 17th century to identify those leaders or writings that could claim some linkage to the original Twelve Apostles, especially John. Typically, the list includes Clement of Rome, Ignatius of Antioch, Polycarp of Smyrna, The Didache, The Shepherd of Hermas, and The Epistle of Barnabas. Some scholars also include Papias, The Epistle of Diogenes, and the Apology of Quadratus as well. The argument is made that these works, being composed by those who had contact with the original apostles, could provide a hermeneutical key to correctly interpreting and understanding the apostolic writings of the NT. See M. H. Shepherd, Jr., "Apostolic Fathers," in *The Interpreter's Dictionary of the Bible*, vol. 1, ed. George A. Buttrick (Nashville, TN: Abingdon Press, 1962, 1982).

the writings (c. 1580) of Theodore Beza, Calvin's successor in Geneva, and proceed to cite subsequent authors whose insights into Scripture begin to undermine the foundations upon which the superstructure of Supersessionism was built. But it is with the advent of Dispensationalism, conceptualized by John Nelson Darby (c. 1830), that we witness the first *systemic* challenge to Supersessionism. I briefly describe what the system is, why it became so popular among many evangelicals, and why it has relatively recently fallen out of favor with the same.

In chapter five, "Begin With the End in Mind," the proposition is set forth that thinking about the end God has in mind for the earth can perhaps help us understand how we are going to get there, i.e., guide us in discerning the overarching narrative and trajectory of Scripture. An emerging theological consensus regarding the final state of affairs posits that God will redeem and restore all of his good creation. There will be a real, material, restored new earth with which heaven will be joined. In "Paradise Restored," there will be rivers, lakes, mountains, vegetation, cities, countryside, animals, and humans. These humans will also be in the form of nations. And one of those nations will be *Israel.* If all of this is true, then it ought to serve as a hermeneutical (interpretive) guide for how we should be reading all of the Scriptures, but especially the NT—in which we will see and understand that God is not "done" with Israel and the Jewish people.

In chapter six, "Getting the Big Story Right," I highlight the fact that Christians have traditionally summarized the grand narrative of the Bible in ways that skip over most of the Tanakh. We see this in the *Apostles' Creed*[15] which starts with God as creator and then jumps to Je-

[15] "For hundreds of years Christians believed that the twelve apostles were the authors of the widely known creed that bears their name. According to an ancient theory, the twelve composed the creed with each apostle adding a clause to form the whole. Today practically all scholars understand this theory of apostolic composition to be legendary. Nevertheless, many continue to think of the creed as apostolic in nature because its basic teachings are agreeable to the theological formulations of the apostolic age. . . . The full form in which the creed now appears stems from about A.D. 700. However, segments of it are found in Christian writings dating as early as the second century. . . . The Apostles' Creed functioned in many ways in the life of the church. For one thing, it was associated with entrance into the fellowship as a confession of faith for those to be baptized. In addition, catechetical instruc-

sus Christ. The same is true with the popular four-word summary: *Creation, Fall, Redemption,* and *Consummation* where *Redemption* is equated with the person and work of Christ. I cite the alliterative form of this summary—*Creation, Curse, Cross,* and *Consummation*—and suggest a *fifth* word beginning with the letter *C* which would address this omission in standard Christian thinking about the Big Story and which needs to be explicitly confessed. That word is *Covenant.* I then proceed to begin teasing out, in broad strokes, the five *C's* of the Big Story. I conclude this chapter dealing with the first two because the traditional understandings of *Creation* and *Curse* do not differ much, if at all, from that which is being posited in the new emerging understanding of the Big Story. But the introduction of the *Covenant* / "Israel and the Nations" theme into the traditional rendition of the Grand Narrative and how that deepens our understanding of the *Cross* and the *Consummation* elements requires separate chapters for each.

In chapter seven, "The Rest of the Story—Covenant," I highlight the fact that God divided rebellious, "generic" humanity by *creating* the *Nations.*[16] This was both a judgment and an act of redemption. It is here that *Covenant* is introduced into the story of God's overarching plan. God establishes a covenant with Abraham that will result in, among other things, creating a new nation *Israel,* which will be distinct from the others, yet exists to be a means of redemption and blessing to the others. This theme of "Israel and the Nations" is woven all throughout the Tanakh and we see many instances of Israel fulfilling its vocation to be a light and a blessing to the Nations. But we also witness the discordant

tion was often based on the major tenets of the creed. In time, a third use developed when the creed became a 'rule of faith' to give continuity to Christian teachings from place to place and to clearly separate the true faith from heretical deviations." – From the articles titled "Creed," "Creeds" (p. 283) and "Apostles' Creed" (p. 72) in the *Evangelical Dictionary of Theology,* ed. Walter A. Elwell (Grand Rapids, MI: Baker Book House, 1984).

16 Throughout this book I will be capitalizing the word *Nation* which is one English equivalent of the underlying Greek word ἔθνος/ *ethnos* from which we get the Anglicized *ethnic.* In most modern translations the capitalized word *Gentiles* is used and with less frequency *nations* or *peoples.* Each translated word has a certain value to its nuance, but for my purposes I want to use the word *Nation* because at the end of the day it is clearer in meaning to most English readers than *Gentiles* and I want to capitalize it as I place it alongside the capitalized word *Israel.*

note of failure through human sin and the prophesied need for a New Covenant and its messenger—the Messiah.

In chapter eight, "The Rest of the Story—Cross," we have the arrival of the Jewish Messiah in the person of Jesus of Nazareth. He does not come to punish or do away with the Jewish people, as though their only purpose for existing was to bring a Messiah into the world and that has now been fulfilled. Rather, he comes to save, redeem, and empower them so that they may truly fulfill their created purpose—to be a blessing to the Nations. And this is exactly what we see unfold in the pages of the NT. Just as in times past Israel had experienced deep divisions—political, geographical, and cultural/spiritual—so now, a major *Messianic* division occurred among the people of God. Fascinatingly, we see both portions of Israel continuing the theme of "Israel and the Nations," but in very different ways.

In chapter nine, "The Rest of the Story—Consummation," I conclude the book with an exposition of the mystery surrounding God's dealings with "Israel and the Nations" as captured in the imagery of *Jesus and the Olive Tree.*

ABOUT THE AUTHOR[17]

While reading J. I. Packer's "Introduction" to his book *Keeping in Step with the Spirit,* I was surprised that such a well-known leader and author in the evangelical world would express the need to describe who he is and where he is coming from theologically. So following his cue, you should know that "I am committed in broad terms to . . . historic Protestant evangelicalism—Bible-based, cross-centered, conversion-oriented, and prioritizing church fellowship and mission outreach."[18]

Furthermore, in both the church where I pastor and HarvestNet Institute where I teach and serve as president, we use *The Lausanne Cove-*

---

17 This section is adapted from my book *The Promise of the Spirit,* xiv–xv, and used by permission.

18 J. I. Packer, *Keep in Step with the Spirit: Finding Fullness in Our Walk with God* (Grand Rapids, MI: Baker Books, 1984, 2005), 10.

nant[19] and *The Chicago Statement on Biblical Inerrancy*[20] as our guiding doctrinal documents. Those familiar with them know that the first is broader and more inclusive in scope and the second is narrower and more exclusive. However, the reader should know that the thesis of this book and its supporting arguments are not directly dependent upon a certain understanding of inerrancy as it relates to Scripture.

Lastly, I think it is important for you to know that I believe there is a *core* to Christianity, an *orthodoxy*, or what C. S. Lewis called *Mere Christianity*. One who is endeavoring to be a faithful follower of Jesus, must not tamper with this deposit of truth but rather "contend for the faith that was once for all delivered to the saints" (Jude 3). But the Scriptures also declare in many places that we as individuals and corporately as the church can and must "grow in the grace and knowledge of our Lord and Savior Jesus Christ" (2 Pet. 3:18). This responsibility has been historically captured in the phrase, *Ecclesia semper reformanda*, Latin for "the church is always to be reformed" and was used as a sort of battle cry of the Protestant Reformation.[21] As Robert M. Bowman, Jr., points out in his book *Orthodoxy and Heresy*, "New heresies and aberrations are constantly arising, as well as new insights into biblical truth, and discernment is needed to tell the difference. Thus, the task of doctrinal discernment is an ongoing necessity in the Christian church."[22] The possibility of promoting "new heresies and aberrations" makes me shutter. But the obligation to recognize the realities that "If anyone imagines that he knows something, he does not yet know as he ought to know"

19 https://www.lausanne.org/content/covenant/lausanne-covenant (accessed on Dec 15, 2015).

20 http://www.alliancenet.org/the-chicago-statement-on-biblical-inerrancy (accessed on Dec 15, 2015).

21 I devote the entirety of chapter nine, "The Challenges of Ecclesia Semper Reformanda," in my previous book *The Promise of the Spirit* to this very important subject.

22 Robert M. Bowman, Jr., *Orthodoxy and Heresy: A Biblical Guide to Doctrinal Discernment* (Grand Rapids, MI: Baker Book House, 1992), p. 56. At the time of writing, Bowman served as special projects editor for the Christian Research Institute, an apologetics ministry which provides "Christians worldwide with carefully researched information and well-reasoned answers that encourage them in their faith and equip them to intelligently represent it to people influenced by ideas and teachings that assault or undermine biblical Christianity and the essentials of the historic Christian faith."

(1 Cor. 8:2) and that we are to "grow up *in every way* into him who is the head, into Christ" (Eph. 4:15)," compels me to humbly share what I believe to be these "new insights into biblical truth" emerging from scholars whose credentials and commitment to the historic Christian faith are beyond question.[23]

A NOTE TO MY JEWISH FRIENDS:

In 2008, I was invited to co-chair an Evangelical-Jewish Dialogue jointly sponsored by the Jewish Federation of Cleveland and HarvestNet Ministries.[24] At the outset of this enterprise I realized how "thin" my knowledge was of the post-temple history of the Jewish people in general and Judaism in particular. So I began peppering my rabbinic colleagues with questions and for reading recommendations on various topics. I will forever be grateful to God and them for their patience, friendship, and guidance in equipping me for my responsibilities in this new role.

Out of these wonderful discussion times with rabbis, pastors, and "lay people" from both communities there arose in 2013 at the suggestion of my rabbinic co-chair a Pastor-Rabbi Roundtable in order to discuss more "theologically"[25] oriented topics. At our meeting in Decem-

---

23 "But one of the serious charges church authorities hurled at the Reformers was that they were 'innovating.' John Calvin responded to this and other charges in his treatise 'The Necessity of Reforming the Church.' As he put it, 'We are accused of rash and impious innovation for having ventured to propose any change at all [in] the former state of the Church.' He then goes on to counter that they were not 'innovating,' but restoring the church to its true nature, purified from the 'innovations' that riddled the church through centuries of inattention to Scripture and theological laxity." Anna Case-Winters, "What do Presbyterians believe about 'Ecclesia Reformata, Semper Reformanda?' Our Misused Motto," *from the May 2004 issue of Presbyterians Today,* http://www.presbyterianmission.org/ministries/today/reformed/ (accessed Jan. 21, 2013).

24 HarvestNet Ministries is an organization composed of evangelical church and marketplace leaders with a common vision to see all of NE Ohio wonderfully renewed by the Gospel. http://www.harvestnetministries.com/ (accessed Sept. 1, 2016).

25 While it is oversimplification to say that historically the Jewish people or what later became known as Judaism focused more on *orthopraxy* (right practice, Heb. *Halakah*) whereas Christianity more on *orthodoxy* (right belief), it still captures something of the existing asymmetry between the two. *Theology* (the study of God) has historically tended to be more of a Christian category. To ask other communities about their "theology" can potentially be viewed as

ber of 2016, I was asked to share for discussion the new emerging paradigm among evangelicals of how to view Jesus and his relationship to the Jewish people. Initially, I had great reservations about the idea.

In my opening remarks, I conveyed to the rabbis present how very difficult it was for me to talk about this subject. In the light of the history of antisemitism in the church and the pain the Jewish people have suffered in the name of Jesus, talking about a new way to think about Jesus and the NT seemed to be adding insult to injury. I couldn't help but imagine that my Jewish friends must think, "If you were really serious about this problem you would abandon the 'Jesus Project.'" (Let me quickly say parenthetically that never once has any of my Jewish friends even hinted at such a suggestion. But I couldn't shake the troubling thought which seemed a very natural, logical conclusion in the light of the history of the church-synagogue relationship.)

I continued by reading Zechariah 8:23 from the JPS translation: *"Thus saith the LORD of hosts: In those days it shall come to pass, that ten men shall take hold, out of all the languages of the nations, shall even take hold of the skirt of him that is a Jew, saying: 'We will go with you, for we have heard that God is with you.'"*[26] Then I commented on the passage by observing, "On September 16, 1973, I 'took hold' of Jesus (although it seems more likely that he took hold of me) and it totally change my life."

I went on to say:

> Now as a human being I have to admit to the possibility that I may have taken hold of the wrong skirt.[27] But in so doing, I have taken hold of you who are seated around this table who have shared invaluable insights with me and through you I have taken hold of authors like Rabbis Daniel Boyarin, Abraham Heschel, Alfred Kolatch, Jacob Neusner, Jonathan Sacks, Joseph B. Soloveitchik, Adin Steinsaltz, Jo-

---

a foreign imposition or even an incomprehensible non sequitur. See also Daniel Boyarin, *Border Lines: The Partition of Judaeo-Christianity* (Philadelphia: Univ. of Penn. Press, 2004), 8.

26 Jewish Virtual Library, "Jewish Publication Society 1917 version of the Tanakh," https://www.jewishvirtuallibrary.org/book-of-zechariah#8, (accessed Dec. 4, 2016).

27 In the language of the philosophers, I have both warrant and justification for my belief, but very few beliefs can reach the threshold of absolute certainty. See Alvin Plantinga, *Warranted Christian Belief* (New York, NY: Oxford University Press, 2000).

seph Telushkin, Michael Wyschogrod, and many others. I can truly say that my faith and biblical understanding have been immeasurably enriched by all of these encounters.

All of this is to say, I am left with a big conundrum. The irony is—had I not had this encounter with Jesus, I would probably be on my fifth marriage and a fifth of Jack Daniels and couldn't give two hoots about all things Jewish. But instead, I am at this table, sharing wonderful friendships with all of you and sharing your concern for the Jewish people and the rise of antisemitism worldwide! Yet, the abominable things that have been done to your people in that name overwhelms me with grief and shame.

So, it seems to me that since it was Jesus who brought me to this "dance," as well as the fact that the 2.4 billion people on the planet who identify with him are probably not going to abandon the "Jesus Project," it would be worth the effort to see if we have missed something in the Scriptures that frames the "Jesus Project" in a way that does not lead to the antisemitism witnessed in the church historically. As one scholar observed in this context, 'The New Testament does not need to be rewritten, but it needs to be reread."[28]

With these opening remarks concluded, I proceeded to share with the Roundtable an outline of what would eventually become the book you have in your hands. After I was finished, I was frankly scared to death in wondering what the reaction would be. To my great relief, it was overwhelmingly positive. Several urged me to put it into book form. This encouragement is in no way to be construed as an endorsement of the "Jesus Project" as such. Rather, it is an expression of appreciation at the attempt to relate it in philosemitic terms.

I need to also say that this initial positive response was to an *outline*. Whether this *book* receives the same positive response remains to be seen. I am in that place of fear and trepidation once again. While the outline I shared with rabbis and pastors at our Roundtable was crafted to a Jewish audience, I have deliberately written this book to a Christian

[28] Dr. Eliyahu Lizorkin-Eyzenberg is president of the Israel Study Center, https://israelstudycenter.com/about-israel-study-center-live-online-classes-from-israel/dr-eli-lizorkin-eyzenberg/ (accessed Dec. 5, 2016).

audience—primarily with pastors and other Christian leaders serving in various domains in mind. This is not a matter of pandering to one audience or another. God forbid! Rather, in each presentation certain points received greater emphasis and elaboration than others, depending upon the interests and concerns of those addressed. I hope that my Jewish friends reading this book are not too disappointed in this new effort or in me.

Why This Subject Is Important

So far, I have basically told you *what this book is about.* I also told you *why I tried to make it relatively short.* But I have not yet explicitly stated *why any of this should matter to you.* Let me do so now:

- **Truth:** Jesus said, "If you abide in my word, you are truly my disciples, and you will know the truth, and the truth will set you free" (John 8:31–32) and "I am the way, the truth, and the life . . . " (John 14:6). If we profess to be following this one, then we must be concerned about truth in all of its dimensions and implications.
- **Falsehood:** To the extent we are not abiding in truth, we hazard entertaining falsehood. Scripture warns us that there is "another Jesus" and a "different gospel" (2 Cor. 11:4) which we are in danger of embracing. Some of the ways that certain portions of the church have historically attempted to separate Jesus from all things Jewish certainly fall into this category and we remain ignorant of this reality to our own peril.
- **Antisemitism:** Sadly, the dynamic of falsehood just mentioned has been a source of antisemitism in the last 2,000 years. Incredibly, this perennial evil is on the rise again worldwide only seventy some years after the Holocaust. Those who embrace the Jewish Messiah of the Jewish Scriptures should be at the forefront of fighting this iniquity—certainly not embracing it.
- **Obedience:** As we come into a fuller, clearer understanding of God's plans for Creation and Redemption, we will be in a better position to do the will of God.

My hope is that this little book will be of help to you in each of these areas of concern.

JESUS AND THE OLIVE TREE

Finally, I would like to direct your attention to the evocative drawing on the cover of this book *Jesus and the Olive Tree* (1940) by Israeli artist Leopold Krakauer.[29] It was included in The Israel Museum - Jerusalem's *Behold the Man: Jesus in Israeli Art* exhibit that featured the works of Jewish artists[30] from the past 100 years who in various ways depicted something about the person Jesus. My wife and I saw a picture of the drawing in an article on the exhibit, knew we had to have it, contacted the current owners, and received permission to use it. I cannot imagine a better way to pictorially capture the essence of what this emerging new paradigm is trying to convey in words. May its depiction of the twisted torso of Jesus—inextricably woven into the very fibers of the Olive Tree representing Israel—help you more fully appreciate the unfolding of the mystery of which you are about to read.

---

[29] Leopold Krakauer (March 1890–December 1954) was an architect and a painter. He was one of the most prominent architects working in Mandate Palestine/Israel in the mid- twenties. He was also a painter who presented drawings and paintings at exhibitions in Israel and all over the world. Krakauer lived in Israel from 1924 until his death.

[30] To my knowledge, none of the artists, including Krakauer, were what are now referred to as Messianic Jews. From the jacket of *Behold the Man: Jesus in Israeli Art* (Jerusalem: Magnes Press, 2017) by Amitai Mendelsohn: "This publication was written to accompany a major exhibition at the Israel Museum that investigates the various appearances of the figure of Jesus in Jewish and Israeli art, revealing a significant, multifaceted, and surprisingly pervasive phenomenon. Surveying works made by prominent artists from different generations, from the second half of the nineteenth century up until today, the richly illustrated text analyzes the evolving attitude of Jewish, Zionist, and Israeli art towards the portrayal of Jesus. This book takes a closer look at artists laboring "in the shadow of the Cross," who saw Jesus as an emblem of the persecuted Jew, as well as artists who saw Jesus as a symbol of the rebirth of the Jewish people in the land of Israel. Also focusing on those who view him as a symbol of the suffering artist and are indifferent to the rocky political relationship between Christianity and Judaism, this clear and straightforward volume is a spectacular addition to every library, and will make a perfect gift for historians, art enthusiasts, and any person who has a thirst for knowledge."

ONE

RE-ENGAGING THE MYSTERY

At the suggestion of a friend of mine who is a Reform rabbi, a roundtable discussion with evangelical pastors and rabbis from various denominations began in the Spring of 2013 in Cleveland, Ohio. At our second meeting, the evangelicals were to share what constitutes "being an evangelical." My task was to locate us within the historical timeline. Rather than reference only the development of the Roman Catholic and Eastern Orthodox expressions of Christianity, for the sake of completeness I decided that I would tangentially mention the "other Christianities."[31] As I did a quick review of that period of church history in which the Christological battles[32] raged (c. 325–451) and from which several of the other Christianities sprung, I was struck afresh with the challenge of "wrestling with mysteries."

It is clear that the *incarnation* is a mystery and the Bible calls it such—"Great indeed, we confess, is the mystery of godliness: He [some MSS read *God*] was manifested in the flesh, vindicated by the Spirit, seen by angels, proclaimed among the nations, believed on in the world, taken up in glory" (1 Tim. 3:16). Therefore, it should not surprise us that human beings had to wrestle with varying constructions of how to

---

[31] Philip Jenkins, *The Lost History of Christianity: The Thousand-Year Golden Age of the Church in the Middle East, Africa, and Asia—and How It Died* (New York: HarperCollins Publishers, 2008).

[32] For an excellent overview of the period and the controversy see Roger E. Olson, *The Story of Christian Theology: Twenty Centuries of Tradition & Reform* (Downers Grove, IL: IVP Academic, 1999), 223–249.

articulate this mystery. It is unfortunate that this controversy was complicated by ecclesial politicking which led to, perhaps, avoidable divisions. But even after carefully arming ourselves with humility, charity, collegiality, and intellectual integrity, all of us who read the Bible seriously are faced with the challenge of engaging with *mystery*.

Mystery Means Mystery

We need to be very clear about the biblical use of the word *mystery*. Some popular definitions that appear in evangelical literature betray a tendency to mute the idea of uncertainty or that which is beyond human comprehension. The following is illustrative:

> As used in the NT, this word doesn't refer to something that is "mysterious" or "cryptic," but rather to something that needs to be revealed by God, in order for us to understand it. These are *revealed* "secrets" from God, which are intended for influencing our lives and attitudes. It may be interesting to note that certain man-made religions have "mysteries" or "secrets," which are revealed only to those who have attained various "levels" in their religious systems. God's "mysteries," however, are open for all who are willing to accept them![33]

A more careful, nuanced definition is given by Stephen Moyter in the *Evangelical Dictionary of Theology*:

> For Paul "mystery" is an important term. Of the twenty-eight NT occurrences twenty-one are from his pen . . . He frequently associates it with words for revelation (e.g., Rom. 16:25; Eph. 3:3-9), and this has led some to assert that, paradoxically, "mystery" is for Paul something no longer mysterious, but clearly revealed. This is certainly true of Eph. 1:9 and Gal. 1:26-27 and accounts for the fact that "mystery" is often virtually identical with "gospel" (e.g., I Cor. 2:1; Eph. 6:19; I Tim. 3:9). Other scholars, however, feel that it must indicate a contin-

---

[33] Dennis Hinks, "NT *Mysteries* or Secrets," ©2001, http://www.journal33.org/other/html/mystery.htm (accessed Nov. 17, 2017).

> uing degree of hiddenness, even if it is part of Paul's revelation vocabulary. Paul does seem to use it to convey the ideas of ultimate ungraspability (e.g., I Cor. 2:7; 13:2; Eph. 5:32; Col. 2:2), or of present incomprehensibility (Rom. 11:25; I Cor. 14:2), or of something eschatological which transcends our present experience (I Cor. 15:51; II Thess. 2:7). These two sides of Paul's usage—revealed and hidden—are not of course contradictory. They correspond to the two facets of all our knowledge of God, whose judgments are unsearchable and ways inscrutable (Rom. 11:33), even though "he had made known to us in all wisdom and insight the mystery of his will" (Eph. 1:9, RSV).[34]

There are ideas or concepts in the Bible that are called *mysteries*. God has revealed them for our instruction and benefit, yet they are ultimately beyond our full comprehension. Over the centuries, theologians have employed lakes of ink and forests of paper wrestling with biblical mysteries: "the mystery of the kingdom of God" (Mark 4:11), "the mystery of Christ" (i.e., about the grafting of Gentiles into the olive tree – Eph. 3:4), "the mystery of the faith" (I Tim. 3:9), "the mystery of godliness" (i.e., about the incarnation – I Tim. 3:16), and even "the mystery of iniquity" (2 Thes. 2:7). This has been a good and appropriate pursuit of truth and understanding—even if at the end of the day we must confess as John Calvin did when after writing about the internal testimony of the Holy Spirit in the life of the believer, "My words fall far beneath a just explanation of the matter."[35]

In fact, many issues in the Bible, not just those specifically labeled as a *mystery*, present us with multifaceted statements that at times can seem almost contradictory and require careful, thoughtful effort to sort through in order to make coherent sense out of them. As if to highlight this reality, since 1987, Zondervan has published a *Counterpoints* series of books dealing with various areas of concern that have occupied the church throughout its history. "Many of the volumes in this unique collection lay out four or five separate views on a theological matter, giving

---

[34] Stephen Moyter, "Mystery," in the *Evangelical Dictionary of Theology*, ed. Elwell, 741–742.

[35] F. H. Klooster, "Internal Testimony of the Holy Spirit," in the *Evangelical Dictionary of Theology*, ed. Elwell, 565.

the reader the chance to weigh the many sides that can arise on a particular issue. All views presented come from extensive research completed by respected biblical scholars and theologians."[36] The following partial listing of titles will give the reader some idea of the scope and nature of the project:

- Five Views on Apologetics
- Five Views on Biblical Inerrancy
- Five Views on Law and Gospel
- Five Views on Sanctification
- Four Views on Eternal Security
- Four Views on the Book of Revelation
- Understanding Four Views on Baptism
- Understanding Four Views on the Lord's Supper
- Four Views on Hell

While it may not be immediately apparent from the titles, those who have some working knowledge of the subjects will recognize that all of these controversies go far back in church history—some as early as the second century. Furthermore, even though none of the topics listed above are called a *mystery* in Scripture, yet as different ones in church history wrestled with them, four or five different views emerged (of course, with varying degrees of merit).

The Neglected Mystery

Yet strangely, there is at least one issue in the Bible, which is clearly defined as a *mystery,* that has not received this kind of detailed attention combined with humility in the history of the church.[37] And that is the

---

[36] Bock, Darrell L.; Grudem, Wayne A.; Strauss, Mark L.; and Bird, Michael F; eds. *The Counterpoints Library: Complete 32-Volume Set: Resources for Understanding Controversial Issues in the Bible, Theology, and Church Life.* Counterpoints: Bible and Theology (Grand Rapids, MI: Zondervan, Paperback, 2015).

[37] In 2003, Zondervan added to its Counterpoints series referenced above a book titled *How Jewish Is Christianity?: Two Views on the Messianic Movement.* This very good book is a major step

mystery of God's dealings with his chosen people Israel: "Lest you be wise in your own sight, I do not want you to be unaware of this **mystery**, brothers: a partial hardening has come upon Israel, until the fullness of the Gentiles has come in" (Rom. 11:25).[38]

As I will describe in more detail later, only *one*, rather simplistic, uncritiqued view of this mystery—Supersessionism or Replacement Theology—emerged early in the history of the church. It remained the unchallenged reigning orthodoxy for 17 centuries until a radical alternative called Dispensationalism arose circa 1830 to challenge it.[39] While arguably in some ways an improvement over Supersessionism, it also (to be charitable) does not do full justice to the Biblical witness.

I titled this chapter "Re-engaging the Mystery" because that is exactly what the church needs to do vis-à-vis "the mystery of Israel." As I stated in the Introduction, this is beginning to happen in our generation.[40] In the remainder of this book, I will attempt to summarize the findings of recent scholarship and lay out an emerging new way of re-engaging this mystery that is more biblically consistent than previous efforts. But first, to understand where we are going, we need to under-

---

in the right direction in that it is dealing with "things Jewish." But the very fact that this book, in contrast to the others in the series, only offers "two views" provides a clue to us that this will not be a comprehensive treatment of the subject of the role of the Jewish people in salvation history. Indeed, as the title and chapter headings indicate, this volume is more narrowly focused on questions surrounding the Messianic Movement and the propriety and role, if any, of Messianic congregations.

38 Of course, I would never affirm something as silly as to say that no one ever addressed this topic or talked about it in church history (e.g., whole works have carried the phrase in their titles; see Increase Mather, *The Mystery of Israel's Salvation, Explained and Applied* (London, 1669); H. L. Ellison, *The Mystery of Israel* (Grand Rapids, MI: The Paternoster Press, 1966). Everything in the Bible has been discussed! I am speaking about the mystery of Israel not being treated with the same level of attention, emphasis, and controversy as other mysteries and doctrinal issues.

39 I am aware of the significant outpouring of literary works produced in the wake of the Reformation that posit a future for the Jewish people and their land, which I address in chapter four. But I am siding with the scholarship which demonstrates it was never put into a *system* that could have wide influence in the church. *Dispensationalism* provided that system.

40 For example, since I began working on this project, two "views" books came out (not by Zondervan) that specifically address this issue: Chad O. Brand, *Perspectives on Israel and the Church: 4 Views* (Nashville, TN: B & H Publishing Group, 2015); Jared Compton and Andrew David Naselli, ed., *Three Views of Israel and the Church: Perspectives on Romans 9–11* (Grand Rapids, MI: Kregel Academic, 2018).

stand how we got to where we are today.

TWO

DEVELOPMENT OR DEVIATION?

While the pages of the Bible contain "some things in them that are hard to understand" (2 Pet. 3:16), not all convey mystery or lead to four or five views as referenced in the last chapter. Thus, we can make several assertions, without controversy, about the *Jewishness* of the NT witness. Jesus was born of a Jewish mother and raised in a Jewish village called Nazareth. Jesus's chosen disciples called apostles or *The Twelve* were all Jewish. When he sent out 70 (some MSS 72) others, they were all Jewish. During the three or so years of his ministry from the time of his baptism by John until his death, he focused almost exclusively on "the lost sheep of the house of Israel" (Matt. 15:24). When teaching, he taught in thought forms that were Jewish. When citing Scriptures, he only referenced the Jewish ones collectively referred to as the Tanakh.

After his resurrection and ascension, the good news of what he had accomplished was proclaimed exclusively to the Jewish people and tens of thousands became his followers. Saul of Tarsus, also called Paul, testifies to the deeply rooted Jewishness of his message before king Agrippa: "I stand here on trial because of my hope in the promise made by God to our fathers, to which our twelve tribes hope to attain, as they earnestly worship night and day" (Acts 26:6–7). It should be noted that he declared this more than 20 years after he became a follower of Jesus, so it cannot be relegated to his "early thinking or understanding." The good news about Israel's Messiah spills over to the Gentiles who begin to follow Jesus and raises a question among the Jewish leaders of the Jesus Movement about what to do with these newcomers to a predominantly Jewish movement. All of the NT documents were written by Jewish men with the likely exception of the two, *Luke* and *Acts*, written by Luke the physician.[41] Finally, the last book of the Bible depicts an eternal state in which a new Jerusalem has twelve gates with the names of the various tribes of Israel inscribed on them (Rev. 21:12).

None of the foregoing is meant to underplay the revolutionary nature of the coming of Israel's Messiah. On the one hand he insisted that he did not "come to abolish the Law or the Prophets," but in the very same breath he added, "I have not come to abolish them but to fulfill them" (Matt. 5:17). His birth, life, miracles, teaching, death, burial, and resurrection would definitively and forever change the future unfolding of Israel's destiny as well as that of the whole world.

But it is absolutely crucial to understand, if we are going to make any coherent sense of the totality of the Bible, that the cosmic change wrought by Christ described in the previous paragraph does not make null the overall Jewish trajectory of the NT narrative. From the genealogy in the first chapter of its first book (Matt. 1), to the Messiah identifying himself as "the descendant of David" in the last chapter of the last book (Rev. 22:16), there is an indelible stamp of Jewishness upon the NT.[42] More on this later.

For now we need to deal with the "curiosity" if not downright "mystery," that within some 70 years after Jesus's resurrection, a significant portion of his followers should begin distancing themselves from all things Jewish. It is to that story we must now turn.

---

41 Some recent scholarship has questioned the traditional view that Luke was a Gentile, but the current weight of the evidence still favors the tradition.

42 One outstanding example among many of the recent scholarly works emphasizing the Jewishness of Jesus and the NT comes from the pen of a modern orthodox Jewish writer: Daniel Boyarin, *The Jewish Gospels: The Story of the Jewish Christ* (New York, NY: The New Press, 2012).

The Dynamics of Departure[43]

In one of his earliest letters, Paul writes: "I am astonished that you are so quickly deserting him who called you in the grace of Christ and are turning to a different gospel" (Gal. 1:6). Most scholars are in agreement that these new Galatian believers in Christ had moved away from the centrality of the Gospel within, perhaps, as little as one year!

Church historian Jeremy Jackson wryly observes, "Although the lapse of time between the Creation and the Fall of man is not specified, the Genesis account makes fairly clear that it was distressingly short," and compares this with "the pressures so quickly brought to bear upon the expanding NT church by inner declension and heresy."[44] Therefore, as we look to the church of the post-apostolic period in the early second century of our era, we should not be too surprised to discover that in rather short order the same dynamic of departure was at work as that which was evident in Galatia. However, now the church as a whole, not just a region (Galatia), had moved away from the centrality of the Gospel.

A Curtain Falls and Rises

All historians of church history, regardless of denominational or doctrinal commitments, comment on and are dismayed by the paucity of information we have about the church from the end of Paul's life in the 60's until the second decade of the second century. Historian J. L. Hurlbut aptly comments, "For fifty years after St. Paul's life a curtain hangs over the Church, through which we strive vainly to look, and when at last it rises . . . we find a Church in many aspects very different from that in the days of St. Peter and St. Paul."[45] Similarly Williston Walker,

---

[43] This section and the next one are adapted from my book *The Promise of the Spirit*, 38–40, and used by permission.

[44] Jeremy C. Jackson, *No Other Foundation: The Church Through Twenty Centuries* (Westchester, IL: Cornerstone Books, 1980), 33.

[45] Jessie L. Hurlbut, *The Story of the Christian Church* (Grand Rapids, MI: Zondervan Publishing House, 1918, 1970), 33.

Professor of Ecclesiastical History at Yale University, states:

> Yet though some gleanings can be recovered from this period, the forty years from 70 to 110 remain one of the obscurest portions of church history. This is the more to be regretted because they were an epoch of rapid change in the church itself. When the characteristics of the church can once more be clearly traced, its general conception of Christianity shows surprisingly little of the distinctive stamp of Paul. Not only must many now unknown missionaries have labored in addition to the great Apostle, but an inrush of ideas from other than Christian sources, brought undoubtedly by converts of heathen antecedents, modified Christian beliefs and practices, especially regarding the sacraments, fastings, and the rise of liturgical forms. The old conviction of the immediacy of the guidance of the Spirit faded, without becoming wholly extinguished. The constitution of the church itself underwent, in this period, a far-reaching development.[46]

Historian Justo Gonzalez concurs when he writes, "not only in their understanding of baptism, but also in their total theological outlook, one senses a distance between the Christianity of the NT—especially that of Paul—and that of the apostolic fathers."[47] Such quotations and observations could be multiplied, but the point is incontrovertible—the church of the second century and on looked quite different from that of the first century. This simple fact requires us to ask, "What are we to make of this?"

Roger Olson, in his excellent *The Story of Christian Theology: Twenty Centuries of Tradition & Reform,* summarizes the trajectory of the second century church from the first as both *digression* and *development*:

> The second century witnessed many changes in Christian thinking about God and salvation. These may be viewed either as a diversion and digression from the message of Jesus and the apostles or as an un-

---

[46] Williston Walker, *A History of the Christian Church* (New York, NY: Charles Scribner's Sons, 1919), 34.

[47] Justo González, *A History of Christian Thought*, vol. 1, *From the Beginnings to the Council of Chalcedon,* rev. ed. (Nashville, TN: Abingdon, 1987), 96.

> folding and development of that message's meaning in new contexts. Perhaps the best way to regard the overall trend in Christian theology throughout the century is as a mixture of both digression and development.[48]

One major digression in theology which took place in the second century and that would have a lasting, deleterious effect on the church was the concerted attempt by the church's primarily Gentile leaders to distance the church from its Hebrew roots. Louis Berkof observes that their teachings concerning the church and its relation to its historic preparation in Israel was not always well understood.[49] On the one hand, we can charitably appreciate their struggle in understanding the connection between God's purposes before and after the coming of Jesus. Indeed, traditional Jewish speculations based on the Talmud regarding the changes that will be wrought with the future coming of the Messiah are at times mixed and tentative. However, there is an undercurrent of anti-Jewishness expressed in the writings of the Apostolic Fathers that is unwarranted and unhealthy. And it is not a stretch to imagine that this followed from their immersion in a culture that was itself highly antisemitic.

Antisemitic Polemics

In *Why The Jews: The Reason for Antisemitism,* Dennis Prager and Joseph Telushkin trace the trajectory of post-Tanakh pagan antisemitism starting in Alexandria Egypt in the third century BCE, through the Hellenist (Greek) culture dominating the Mediterranean world of the first two centuries prior to the common era, and culminating in the Roman Empire. After quoting several examples of Roman disdain for Jews, they cite the great Jewish historian Salo Baron who summarized by observing that "almost every note in the cacophony of medieval and modern anti-

---

48 Olson, *The Story of Christian Theology,* 79.

49 Louis Berkof, *The History of Christian Doctrines* (Grand Rapids, MI: Baker Book House, 1937, 1975–paperback), 227.

semitism was sounded by the chorus of ancient writers."[50] It would seem almost impossible that this milieu of pagan antisemitism would leave the church, increasingly comprised of Gentiles who had recently come out of such an environment, unscathed. Indeed, Paul Johnson, in his *A History of the Jews*, unequivocally affirms that the church as a whole, and the Greek [eastern] church in particular, "inherited the whole corpus of pagan Hellenistic antisemitism."[51] Unfortunately for Jew and Gentile alike, this animus infected the writings of the church fathers vis-à-vis the church and the Jewish people.

Gerald McDermott highlights another reality that led to the anti-Jewish polemics of these second century church leaders:

> In the mid-second century, when the synagogue was still very attractive to many Jesus-believing Jews and Gentiles, some of the former were tempted to jettison their new devotion to Jesus, and some of the latter were drawn to non-messianic Judaism. Early church leaders responded by stressing the superiority of Jesus' law to the Mosaic law. Their apologetic against the synagogue was so successful that their new version of salvation history—which declared that God had transferred the covenant from Israel to the church—became dominant.[52]

The church of this period faced the legitimate challenge of trying to explain how this new entity called the body of Messiah/Christ, which was initially composed of a significant minority of the Jewish population and now increasingly of Gentiles, was to be compared and contrasted with the remaining larger portion of the Jewish community in the light of the Tanakh. But inherited cultural antisemitism and competition with the synagogues inevitably colored and distorted their efforts. Popular leadership guru John Maxwell's maxim: "Everything rises and falls on lead-

---

[50] Dennis Prager and Joseph Telushkin, *Why The Jews: The Reason for Antisemitism* (New York: A Touchstone Book, 1983, 2003), 68–73.

[51] Paul Johnson, *A History of the Jews* (New York: Harper and Row, Publishers, 1987), 165.

[52] Gerald R. McDermott, "A History of Supersessionism: Getting the Big Story Wrong," in *The New Christian Zionism: Fresh Perspectives on Israel and the Land*, ed. Gerald R. McDermott (Downers Grove, IL: IVP Academic, 2016), 35–36.

ership" certainly played itself out in this critical, formational period of church history. In the next chapter, we give a brief overview of the development of this anti-Jewishness into Supersessionism or Replacement Theology.

THREE

JETTISONING THE JEWISH CONNECTION

In this chapter we will attempt to give an overview of how the church jettisoned its Jewish connection. The following does not pretend to be a comprehensive treatment of anti-Jewish sentiments among the church fathers,[53] which, unfortunately, was nearly universal. Rather, for the purposes of this brief treatise, I will highlight only a few that mark milestones in its development. I begin with some of the writings from what is known collectively as the Apostolic Fathers.

THE DIDACHE

The *Didache*, otherwise known as *The Teaching of the Twelve Apostles*, is one of the oldest[54] of these materials. Though the actual author is unknown, the first line reads: "The teaching of the Lord to the Gentiles (or Nations) by the twelve apostles." This brief treatise, designed to be used as a catechism for new believers, shows some early signs of anti-Jewish sentiments.

---

[53] The amount of scholarly material on the subject of anti-Jewish sentiments among the church fathers is enormous. Examples include: Dunn, James D. G., *Jews and Christians: The Parting of the Ways, AD 70 to 135.* Grand Rapids, MI: Wm. B. Eerdmans Publishing, 1999; Flannery, Edward H. *The Anguish of the Jews: Twenty-Three Centuries of Antisemitism.* Mahwah, NJ: Paulist Press,1985; Johnson, Paul. *A History of the Jews.* New York: Harper and Row, Publishers, 1987.

[54] The consensus of modern scholarship believes it is a composite work and dates the earliest portions at c. 100.

For example, in chapter eight[55] verse one we read: "But let not your fasts be with the hypocrites; for they fast on the second and the fifth day of week; but do ye fast on the fourth *day* and the Preparation (Friday)." The reasons for fasting on Wednesday and Friday are given in the *Apostolic Constitutions*[56] (the days of betrayal and of burial). Jesus certainly taught his primarily Jewish audience that they should not be like the hypocrites when they fast—not by avoiding the same days on which they fasted, but rather by doing so in secret (Matt. 6:16–18). On the contrary, since the second and fifth days of the week (Mondays and Thursdays) were the Jewish fast days, this directive lumped all Jewish people as hypocrites, not to mention Jewish followers of Jesus[57] (hereafter JFJ) who fasted on these days as well.

In a similar manner, verse two goes on to exhort: "Neither pray as the hypocrites; but as the Lord commanded in His Gospel, this pray: 'Our Father who art in heaven'..." After recounting the full prayer, the chapter ends in verse three with, "Thrice in the day thus pray." It was the custom of observant Jewish people then as now to pray the *Amida* three times a day. This exhortation again lumps all Jewish people as hypocrites (again including the JFJ) and yet attempts to copy the Jewish people as if to say, "Oh, so the Jewish people are telling us that a mark of being one of God's people is praying three times a day. Well, *we* will pray three times a day also, but we will use 'the correct' prayer formula" (Matt. 6:5–6).

55 Isaac H. Hall and John T. Napier, "The Teaching of the Twelve Apostles," in *The Ante-Nicene Fathers: The Writings of the Fathers Down to A.D. 325*, vol. 7, ed. Alexander Roberts & James Donaldson, (Grand Rapids, MI: Eerdmans, 1956), 379.

56 A later work, portions of which are drawn from *The Didache*.

57 Here I am following Boyarin and other recent scholars, who urge abandoning the use of the problematic and anachronistic term "Jewish Christians." Daniel Boyarin, "Rethinking Jewish Christianity: An Argument for Dismantling a Dubious Category (To Which Is Appended a Correction of My Borderlines)." Jewish Quarterly Review (2009) 99: 7–36; cited in Isaac W. Oliver, "Jewish Followers of Jesus and the Bar Kokhba Revolt: Reexamining the Christian Sources," (2009), http://www.academia.edu/2123957/Jewish_Followers_of_Jesus_and_the_Bar_Kokhba_Revolt_Re-examining_the_Christian_Sources (accessed May 10, 2018).

IGNATIUS

Church history identifies the apostolic father Ignatius (c. 35 or 50? to c. 117) as the third bishop of Antioch and a student of the apostle John. Tradition has it that he wrote seven letters to various churches en route to his martyrdom in Rome. These letters contain some concepts that clearly represent digressions from the content of the NT among which is Ignatius's attempt to distance the things pertaining to Jesus from their historic Jewish context.

We start with this provocative statement in his *Epistle to the Magnesians*: "It is absurd to speak of Jesus Christ with the tongue, and to cherish in the mind a Judaism which had now come to an end. For where there is Christianity there cannot be Judaism" (Magnesians 10:3).[58] Although the NT speaks of Christ as "the end (Gk. *telos:* end, goal, purpose) of the law for righteousness" (Rom. 10:4), nowhere does it indicate that Christ is the end of the Jewish people or all things Jewish.

But there is a further complication lurking here. It seems that Ignatius first coins a new term "Christianity"[59] (Gk. χριστιανισμός) in order to juxtapose it with his own distinctive definition of the word "Judaism" (Gk. Ἰουδαϊσμός). Then, as Klaus Wengst points out, "in Ignatius of Antioch's Letter to the Magnesians (9:1), the celebration of the Sabbath and life according to the Lord's Day are set in contrast to each other....Throughout his work 'living in accordance with Christianity' means standing in contrast to 'living Jewishly' (Magnesians 10:13). He already connects this with a model of the replacement of Judaism by Christianity. 'Christianity,' he writes, 'has not believed in Judaism, but Judaism in Christianity, into which each tongue that has come to believe has been gathered.'"[60]

---

58 Ignatius, "Epistle of Ignatius to the Magnesians," in *The Ante-Nicene Fathers*, vol. 1, 63.

59 Ignatius not only uses Χριστιανός [Christian] as a designation but also uses the term as an adjective ('Christian food' in Ign. Trall. 6:1) and uses the related noun χριστιανισμός [Christianity]; this is the first use of this term in Christian literature and it may have been coined by Ignatius, or perhaps by others in Antioch. – Paul Trebilco, *Self-designations and Group Identity in the NT* (Cambridge, UK: Cambridge Univ. Press, 2012), 287.

60 Klaus Wenntt, "When Did Christianity Originate?" posted 01.12.2003 on the International Council of Christians and Jews website http://www.jcrelations.net/When+Did+ Christiani-

The Epistle of Barnabas

Catholic writer Thomas Mirus summarizes the anti-Jewish tone of parts of the work known to us as *The Epistle of Barnabas*:[61]

> The author's interpretation of the Old Testament and the Jewish Law is also far removed from that of St. Paul, whom St. Barnabas accompanied on his travels. In the Pauline view, the Old Law, while it had no salvific power in itself, was nonetheless divinely ordained and paved the way for Christ who fulfilled and replaced the old regulations with the New Covenant.
>
> The author of the Epistle of Barnabas, on the other hand, claims that the literal interpretation of the Mosaic Law by the Jews was a complete misunderstanding; he goes so far as to compare Jewish worship with pagan worship and says that the Jews took the Law literally "because an evil angel deluded them." He also claims that the Old Law was intended not for Jews, but for Christians from the beginning. Much of the Epistle is therefore dedicated to showing the true spiritual meaning of the Old Law by allegorical interpretation.

Justin Martyr

As is clear from the aforementioned writings of these Apostolic Fathers, we witness troubling and biblically unjustifiable *statements* regarding the Jewish people. In the generation after them beginning with Justin Martyr (c. 100–165), we find, not mere *statements*, but *an entire treatise* that clearly articulates in nascent form the paradigm of Supersessionist or Replacement theology. Titled *Dialogue with Trypho*[62] (c. 155–165), we are

---

ty+Originate%3F.2788.0.html?L=3 (accessed Jan. 13, 2018). Paper given at the first Ecumenical Kirchentag, Berlin 2003. Source: *Begegnungen. Zeitschrift für Kirche und Judentum*, Nr. 3, 2003. Translation from the German: Fritz Voll with editing by Franklin Sherman. See also Boyarin, *Border Lines*, 8.

61 Occasionally jumbled and incoherent in structure, the Epistle of Barnabas is neither an epistle nor written by Barnabas. In Chapter XVI it is made clear that the text was written after the destruction of Jerusalem in 70, which Barnabas did not survive.... Modern scholars tend to date the Epistle to the period 117–132. Thomas V. Mirus, *The Didache*, https://www.catholicculture.org/commentary/articles.cfm?id=628 posted on Aug. 19, 2014 (accessed Jan. 19, 2018).

62 Justin Martyr, "Dialogue with Trypho," in *The Ante-Nicene Fathers*, vol. 1, 194–270.

invited to a discussion between the author and a real or more probably hypothetical Jewish skeptic. In it, Justin postulates that God used the Jewish people, i.e., Israel of old, to bring the Messiah into the world. Once that purpose was accomplished, God had no more use for this natural ethnic people-group. Whatever promises were made to them have already been fulfilled in the past or are fulfilled in Christ. The church is now the "true spiritual Israel"[63] who now inherits all of the promises and blessings of God by virtue of being "in Christ."

> As Patristic scholar Robert Lewis Wilken points out, a turning point in the dialogue between Trypho and Justin came when the Jewish thinker realized that they had two divergent views of Israel. While Trypho assumed "Israel" refers only to descendants of Abraham, according to the flesh, he asked Justin "What is this? Are you Israel and is he speaking these things about you?" To this, Justin answered in the affirmative. Justin identifies Israel with Jesus, literally translating "Israel" as the one who overcomes in power, a name merited by Jesus alone.[64]

Furthermore, in chapter 18 Justin strangely declares: "For we too would observe the fleshly circumcision, and the Sabbaths, and in short all the feasts, if we did not know for what reason they were enjoined to you,—namely, on account of your transgressions and the hardness of your hearts."[65] This is not just a "one off" statement, but is repeated in a variety of ways throughout the treatise. Jesus, on only one occasion that we know of, said, "Because of your hardness of heart Moses allowed you to divorce your wives, but from the beginning it was not so" (Matt. 19:8). Contrariwise, Justin seems to imply that most of the injunctions of the Torah were given for this reason, thereby wrongly impugning the law as well as the Jewish people as a whole.

---

[63] Ibid., 200. To scholars' current knowledge, this is the first time this term is ever used by anyone.

[64] Russel D. Moore, "The Doctrine of Last Things" in *A Theology for the Church*, ed. Daniel L. Akin (Nashville, TN: H & B Publishing Group, 2007), 876, citing Robert L. Wilken, "In Novissimis Diebus: Biblical Promises, Jewish Hopes, and Early Christian Exegesis," in *Journal of Early Christian Studies 1* (1993): 15.

[65] Justin Martyr, "Dialogue with Trypho," 203.

IRENAEUS

Writing about a generation later, Irenaeus reinforces and develops themes introduced in Justin's *Dialogue.* Gerald McDermott succinctly relates Irenaeus's contribution to the jettisoning of the Jewish connection to the Gospel:

> Irenaeus's grand metaphor was God as pedagogue. He gave the Mosaic law to the "headstrong" Jews because they needed it for their spiritual education; it was not for all times and all places. Their prescriptions were "temporal," "carnal' and "earthly," calling their users to another law that is "eternal," "spiritual" and "heavenly." Many precepts were included in the old law because of the Jews' "hardness of heart."
>
> After the Jewish law, the incarnation was the next stage in God's pedagogy of the human race. God used it to bring us into his very being, by what Irenaeus called "recapitulation." By this he meant that God started over again on the creation. Because Adam's sin significantly marred the divine image in humanity and prevented the Father from being able to bring human beings into communion with himself, he created the perfect man in Jesus—the man Adam was intended to be. Because Jesus was perfect, without sin, the Father could have communion with him. And because Jesus' human nature was *human*, like ours, we could have communion with God—because Jesus' human nature was the go between that now linked us with God.
>
> This was all very elegant. But it made the history of Israel, which made up most of the Bible, functionally and theologically unnecessary. It suggested that the story of Israel was simply educational, teaching the Gentiles how *not* to proceed, thus preparing the rest of us for the Second Adam. Hence it was *economic* supersessionism. Because it made Israel unnecessary, skipping from the first Adam directly to the Second, it was also *structural* supersessionism. Irenaeus also made use of *punitive* supersessionism by arguing that because the Jews repudiated their Messiah, they were "disinherited from the grace of God."[66]

---

[66] Gerald R. McDermott, "A History of Supersessionism: Getting the Big Story Wrong," in *The New Christian Zionism*, 37–38. McDermott's quotes come from Irenaeus, "Against Heresies," in Philip Schaff, *Apostolic Fathers with Justin Martyr and Irenaeus*, vol. 1 of *The Ante-Nicene Fathers*, eds. Roberts and Donaldson, 4.14., 4.15.1–2.

Kendal Soulen adds this important insight regarding Irenaeus: "Irenaeus . . . seems to have had little knowledge of the Tetragrammaton [the four Hebrew letters that comprise the sacred name of God, not pronounced by the Jewish people and usually read as *Adonai* or translated as *LORD*] and its place in the Scriptures he sought to interpret. I think this lack contributed greatly to the supersessionistic form his canonical narrative took, a bit like scurvy is caused by a deficiency of vitamin C."[67]

The Die Is Cast

With the writings of Justin and Irenaeus we may fairly observe that the die had been cast for all future articulations of the role of Israel, i.e., the Jewish people, in God's unfolding plans for the world. Future writers would follow their general lead with added darker signature embellishments as demonstrated in the following examples.

Bishop Melito of Sardis in his tract *Peri Pascha* (On the Pascha–c. 167), made assertions that transformed the charge that the Jewish people had killed their own Messiah into the charge that they had killed God himself. "God put to death! the king of Israel slain with Israel's right hand! Alas for the new wickedness of the new murder!"[68] Ironically, Melito was Jewish by birth.

Origen (185–254) wrote in his commentary on Matthew (c. 246–248): "Therefore the blood of Jesus was not only blamed upon them, who were alive then, but also on every generation of the Jews following after, until the end of the world." To date, the consensus of scholarship believes this to be the first explicit articulation of a "theology of collective guilt"—the assignment of guilt to all Jewish people for all time for

---

67 R. Kendall Soulen, "The Standard Canonical Narrative and the Problem of Supersessionism," in *Introduction to Messianic Judaism: Its Ecclesial Context and Biblical Foundations*, eds. David Rudolph and Joel Willitts (Grand Rapids, MI: Zondervan, 2013), 285–286. Soulen continues in this chapter to outline how Irenaeus's canonical narrative (which has dominated church history since it was first introduced), can be invigorated while excising its unnecessary supersessionist aspects.

68 Melito of Sardis, "Melito, The Philosopher," in *The Ante-Nicene Fathers*, vol. 8, 757.

the death of Jesus, rather than to some of the leaders of the Jewish community in first century Jerusalem.[69]

St. John Chrysostom (c. 349–407) in 386-7, gave a series of eight sermons which were published in a work titled *Against the Jews* (Gk. Kata Ioudaiōn; L. Adversus Judaeos). He set a new low in hurling invectives against the Jewish people, expanding on the theme of deicide introduced by Melito and concluding that for such a crime there was no expiation, pardon or indulgence possible.[70] Anglican scholar of Jewish-Christian relationships James Parkes describes it as "the most horrible and violent denunciations of Judaism to be found in the writings of a Christian theologian."[71] Recently, attempts have been made by some scholars to ameliorate the "Golden-mouthed" (Gk. Chrysostom) orator's vitriol by saying his writings were aimed at the Christians in his congregation who had gone astray with their fascination with the synagogue and that his attacks on the Jewish people were only secondary and in keeping with "the period's fiery rhetorical customs." The following few select lines from *Homily One* will give readers an idea of the "feast" in store for them if they are intrepid enough to read all eight homilies:

> "Who should not make bold to declare plainly that the synagogue is a dwelling of demons? God is not worshipped there. Heaven forbid! From now on it remains a place of idolatry" {3:3} . . . "They live for their bellies, they gape for the things of this world, their condition is not better than that of pigs or goats because of their wanton ways and excessive gluttony. They know but one thing: to fill their bellies and be drunk" {4:1} . . . For, tell me, is not the dwelling place of demons a place of impiety even if no god's statue stands there? Here the slayers of Christ gather together, here the cross is driven out, here God is

---

69 Roger Pearse, "Origen on Matthew 27:25 from the Commentariorum in Matthaeum Series," posted on June 10, 2015 https://www.roger-pearse.com/weblog/2015/06/10/origen-on-matthew-2725-from-the-commentariorum-in-matthaeum-series/ (accessed on Nov. 28, 2018).

70 Edward H. Flannery, *The Anguish of the Jews*, 52.

71 James Parkes, *Prelude to Dialogue: Jewish Christian Relationships* (London: Schocken Books, 1969), 153.

> blasphemed, here the Father is ignored, here the Son is outraged, here the grace of the Spirit is rejected. Does not greater harm come from this place since the Jews themselves are demons? {6:3} . . . So the godlessness of the Jews and the pagans is on a par. But the Jews practice a deceit which is more dangerous. In their synagogue stands an invisible altar of deceit on which they sacrifice not sheep and calves but the souls of men" {6:4}.[72]

Obviously, this ever-growing "canon" of warped views of the Jewish people by Gentile church leaders greatly contributed to the jettisoning of the Jewish connection to the church and thus reinforced the doctrinal construct of Supersessionism. Additionally, the move away from a millennial understanding of a future reign of the Messiah on the earth reinforced this view of eschatology. Louis Berkhof nicely summaries the dynamics for us:

> The Millennarianism of the early Church was gradually overcome. When centuries rolled by without the return of Jesus Christ, when persecutions ceased, and when Christianity received a sure footing in the Roman Empire and even became the State religion, the passionate longing for the appearance of Jesus Christ very naturally gave way for an adaption of the Church to its present task. The allegorical interpretation of Scripture, introduced by the Alexandrian school, and sponsored especially by Origen, also had a chilling effect on all millennial hopes. In the West the powerful influence of Augustine was instrumental in turning the thoughts of the Church from the future to the present by his identification of the Church and the Kingdom of God. He taught the people to look for the millennium in the present Christian dispensation.[73]

It is not too much of a stretch to say that the hermeneutical supersession of the allegorical method of interpretation over the historical-

---

[72] John Chrysostom, "Against the Jews," The Council of Centers on Jewish-Christian Relations, http://www.ccjr.us/dialogika-resources/primary-texts-from-the-history-of-the-relationship/247-chrysostom#homily1 (accessed Mar. 6, 2018).

[73] Berkof, *The History of Christian Doctrines*, 262–263.

grammatical[74] method led to the theological supersession of any concept of covenantal land promises being fulfilled in the age to come. This, combined with the writings of the church fathers and the official decrees of the "Christianized" Roman state against the Jewish people, led to the completion of the supersessionist project, i.e., the replacement of a Jewish people in a Promised Land (with the Nations in harmony with Israel and one another) by a Gentile church in a promised heaven.

The Jewish Contribution

While the lion's share of responsibility for why and how the church jettisoned its Jewish connection falls primarily upon the Gentile leadership of the church of the second through fourth centuries, our brief survey must include the contribution played by the leadership of the Jewish community who did not accept the Messianic claims of Jesus.[75] Two developments in particular deserve our attention—the "blessing" against heretics and the Jewish revolts.

The "Blessing" Against the Heretics: In 70, Yochanan ben Zakkai and other leaders formed a center of Jewish study in the town of Yavneh near Joppa to undertake the daunting task of reconstituting Jewish practice in the light of the destruction of the temple in Jerusalem. While it is difficult to pin down exact dates, sometime towards the end of the first century or into the second, what amounted to a curse upon heretics was added to the *Amida*, the prayer all devout Jewish people pray three times a day, that would make it impossible for the JFJ to continue worshiping in the synagogues with their countrymen. Rabbi Jack Abramowitz explains the reasoning:

> The twelfth bracha, against heretics, is the one that was later inserted,

---

[74] I know I am using these technical terms anachronistically and not precisely, but with them I can make the general point concisely.

[75] While a number of good works are available on the parting of the ways between the church and the synagogue, Boyarin's *Borderlines* provides a recent, nuanced, and extensive treatment. Boyarin, Daniel. *Borderlines: The Partition of Judaeo-Christianity*. Philadelphia, PA: Univ. of Penn. Press, 2004.

> with the result that there are nineteen blessings in the "Eighteen Benedictions." According to the Talmud in Brachos (28b), this blessing was added in the days of Rabban Gamliel in response to an increase in heretics. According to Rashi there, "minim" (heretics) refers to those who deny the Divine origin of the Torah. The term minim is commonly, though not exclusively, used by the Talmud to refer to early Christian sects, who were more comparable to today's "Messianic Jews" than to modern Christianity. (That is, they identified as Jews, albeit with ideas anathema to Jewish thought, rather than as a fully-independent religion.) Since this philosophy posed a threat to the nation, the bracha was instituted as an anti-missionary move. It refers, however, to any individual or group espousing heretical ideas within the community, such as the Sadducees. (In fact, it is the Sadducees who are mentioned by name in the Talmud where Rabban Gamliel requests that such a bracha be composed, though this may be a later edit.)[76]

It should be noted that a somewhat parallel "prayer" for "the perfidious Jews" found its way into the Roman Catholic liturgy.[77]

The Jewish Revolts: During the Jewish revolt against the Romans in 70, there is good evidence[78] which suggests that the JFJ heeded Jesus's warning to flee Jerusalem when they saw that it was surrounded by armies (Lk. 21:20–21). This action was viewed as community betrayal by the greater Jewish population.

---

76 Jack Abramowitz, "Bracha #12 – Birkas HaMinim (Heretics)," Orthodox Union https://www.ou.org/torah/tefillah/shemoneh-esrei/shemoneh_esrei_12/ (accessed Mar. 28, 2018).

77 "The theology of contempt found its way into the Christian liturgy. The Good Friday liturgy of the Roman Missal contained a prayer for 'the perfidious Jews' and asked God to 'withdraw the veil from their hearts that they may acknowledge our Lord Jesus Christ.' Pope John XXIII abolished this prayer in 1965 during the Second Vatican Council. But the centuries had taken their toll.' Anthony Julius, Robert S. Rifkind, Jeffrey Weill, and Felice D. Gaer, "ANTISEMITISM: An Assault on Human Rights," (Jacob Blaustein Institute for the Advancement of Human Rights, 2001) https://www.ajc.org/anti-semitism-an-assault-on-human-rights (accessed on Feb. 9, 2018).

78 J. Julius Scott, "Did Jerusalem Christians Flee to Pella?" Archaeology Conference, Wheaton College, Wheaton, IL (1998) https://www.preteristarchive.com/Bibliography/1998_scott_flee-pella.html (accessed May 4, 2018).

The Second[79] or Bar Kokhba Revolt (132–135) decisively affected the relationship between the JFJ and the broader Jewish community negatively. Rabbi Akiva, arguably one of the most influential rabbis of the day, surnamed the leader of the revolt Shimon ben Kosevah, *bar Kokhba,* meaning "Son of the Star" in Aramaic—a reference to the Messianic prophecy in Num. 24:17. This would obviously be a non-starter for JFJ. According to Justin Martyr and the early church historian Eusebius, Bar Kokhba severely punished many of them for their refusal to fight with him against the Romans.[80]

Obviously, these developments greatly contributed to the separating of the JFJ from the broader Jewish community as well as provided fodder for the growing Gentile portion of the Jesus Movement to distance themselves from all things Jewish.

THE ROMAN CONTRIBUTION

Finally, for completeness sake, we must briefly mention the contributions of the Roman emperors to the church's jettisoning of its Jewish connection.

The Jewish Tax: In the wake of the destruction of the temple, the Roman Emperor Vespasian imposed a tax (*fiscus Iudaicus*) on all Jewish people, including women and children, the proceeds of which were to go for the maintenance of the Temple of Jupiter Capitolinus in Rome. At the time, Jesus followers would have been considered just another sect of the Jewish people. However, at some point not too long after its implementation, certain Christians petitioned the Emperor to distinguish the Christians for the purpose of the payment of the *fiscus Iudaicus.*

---

[79] Some scholars refer to the turbulent activity in the years 115–117 (Kitos War) as the Second Revolt and Bar Kokhba's as the Third, but I am following the majority. See Wikipedia, "Kitos War," https://en.wikipedia.org/wiki/Kitos_War (accessed May 1, 2018).

[80] Isaac W. Olivera, "Jewish Followers of Jesus and the Bar Kokhba Revolt: Re-examining the Christian Sources," (2009) https://www.academia.edu/2123957/Jewish_Followers_of_Jesus_and_the_Bar_Kokhba_Revolt_Re-examining_the_Christian_Sources (accessed May 10, 2018).

In essence, they were asking to be recognized as a separate religion.[81]

Constantine: Later, Constantine's rise to power over Rome in the wake of his "conversion" to Christianity in 312, signalled a major bellwether change in the history of the world, the church, and the synagogue. As the once-Christian-persecuting empire began issuing decrees favorable to the church, it simultaneously began passing laws unfavourable to the Jewish people which would have long-lasting consequences. As Chaim Potok observed, "The successor of Constantine, his son Constantius, regarded the Jews as a 'despicable sect.' That term would soon become a permanent addition to the vocabulary of western man."[82]

Amazingly, in spite of this conspiracy of contributions to distance the Jesus Movement from all things Jewish, significant numbers of Jewish people continued to self-identify as Jews *and* as followers of Jesus even as late as the early fifth century of this era.[83] But the institutional, primarily Gentile church, was set on a simple, unquestionable commitment to Supersessionism/Replacement Theology in which anything Jewish had no place.[84] It would not be challenged in any significant way until after the Protestant Reformation. To this next part of our story we now turn.

---

81 Shaye J. D. Cohen, review of *The Fiscus Judaicus and the Parting of the Ways*, by Marius Heemstra (Tubingen: Mohr Siebeck, 2010) for the Biblical Archaeology Society (10/10/2012) https://www.biblicalarchaeology.org/reviews/the-fiscus-judaicus-and-the-parting-of-the-ways/ (accessed May 4, 2018).

82 Chaim Potok, *Wanderings: History of the Jews* (New York: Ballantine Books, 1978), 309.

83 Jerome, in a letter to Augustine, references the *Nazarenes* who are to be found "in all the synagogues of the East among the Jews" and that they consider themselves both Christians and Jews, but Jerome says they are neither. *Jerome's Letter to Augustine* (Letter 75– A.D. 404) 4:13, http://www.newadvent.org/fathers/1102075.htm (accessed May 10, 2018).

84 "Still today a famous German New Testament professor can say (as he did) to his students: 'If you want to be a good Christian, you must kill the Jew in your heart.' I quote this professor's words not because I am a Jew, but because he used the word 'kill' as if it were a Christian virtue. Furthermore, the opinion that 'you have to kill the Jew in your heart' is not unconnected with an important trend that existed in Christianity from its beginnings." David Flusser, "Introduction," in Elmer A. Josephson, *Israel, God's Key to World Redemption* (Ottawa, KS: Bible Light Intl., 1974) cited on Jerusalem Perspective, https://www.jerusalemperspective.com/4645/ (accessed Dec. 4, 2018).

FOUR

Dispensing With Dispensationalism

In the previous chapter we embarked on a brief survey of how the church of the second and third centuries jettisoned its Jewish connection by developing a hermeneutical grid through which to view God's purposes for the Jewish people/Israel and the church which resulted in what has come to be called Supersessionism, Replacement Theology, or more recently, Fulfillment Theology. The church, primarily Gentile in nature, has superseded or replaced the Jewish people as the people of God and is now the "true Israel." This view, which is still widely held in Roman Catholic, Eastern Orthodox, and many Protestant expressions of Christianity, reigned through the history of the church as an unchallenged,[85] almost self-evident truth until shortly after the Protestant Reformation.

Reformational Reconsiderations

The advent of the Protestant Reformation (c. 1517) and its emphasis on *ad fontes* (to the sources) encouraged fresh study of the Tanakh in He-

[85] "There were exceptions, however: Hildegard of Bingen [1098–1179] forecast a period of peace and the conversion of the Jews before the return of Christ. Joachim of Fiore (ca. 1135–1202) and many later theologians influenced by him predicted the mass conversion of Jews in a future age of the Spirit....Gerard of Borgo San Donnino (ca. 1255) said that some Jews would be blessed as Jews in the end time, and they would return to their homeland. John of Rupescissa (ca. 1310–1366) said Jews would be converted and Jerusalem would be rebuilt to become the center of a renewed and purified faith. It was not until the Reformation and later, however, that renewed vision for a future Israel gained momentum." McDermott, *The New Christian Zionism,* 56.

brew. "Not only did these Hebraists study the Old Testament in Hebrew and Aramaic, but they also read the comments on it by the various Rabbis, many of whom predicted a glorious future on earth for the Jews."[86]

Further, the general trend to abandon the Medieval hermeneutic known as the *quadriga*[87] in favor of the *sensus literalis* or grammatical-historical reading of Scripture led a number of interpreters to see an abiding relevance, not only of the Jewish people, but of the land of Israel in the economy of God. Several scholars[88] have chronicled these developments and there is now a wealth of historical information available to the interested reader. However, as with our survey of the early church, for the sake of space I will only reference those writers whose contributions represent somewhat original and significant interpretive developments.

A FUTURE FOR THE PEOPLE OF ISRAEL

Theodore Beza (1519–1605), successor to Calvin in leading the Protestant Reformation in Geneva, was the first of the Reformers to discern within the pages of the NT that God was not finished with the Jewish people. Peter Toon, in the preface to *Puritans, the Millennium, and the Future of Israel,* in a concise way gives us the 16th century theological / es-

---

86 Peter Toon, ed. *Puritans, the Millennium, and the Future of Israel: Puritan Eschatology 1600 to 1660* (Cambridge, England: James Clarke & Co. 1970, 2002), 23.

87 Quadriga (literally–team of four): The four-fold method of interpreting the Scriptures: (1) literal – plain and evident meaning, e.g., Jerusalem – capital of Judea (the central sanctuary of the nation) (2) moral – instructed men how to behave, e.g., Jerusalem – the soul of man (the "central sanctuary" of man) (3) allegorical – the content of faith, e.g., Jerusalem – the church (the center of the Christian community) (4) anagogical – expressed future hope, e.g., Jerusalem – heaven (the final hope of future residence for the people of God). R. C. Sproul, *Knowing Scripture* (Downers Grove, IL: InterVarsity Press, 1977), 54.

88 See Daniel C. Juster, *Passion For Israel: A Short History of the Evangelical Church's Commitment to the Jewish People and Israel* (Clarksville, MD; Lederer Books, 2012); Franz Kobler, *The Vision Was There. A History of the British Movement for the Restoration of the Jews to Palestine* (London: World Jewish Congress, 1956); McDermott, "A History of Christian Zionism," in *The New Christian Zionism;* Peter Toon, ed., Puritans, the Millennium, and the Future of Israel; William C. Watson, *Dispensationalism Before Darby: Seventeenth-Century and Eighteenth-Century English Apocalypticism* (Silverton, OR: Lampion Press LLC, 2015).

chatological landscape into which Beza made his contribution:

> The first reformers of the sixteenth century, be they Lutheran or Reformed, adopted the traditional Augustinian eschatology. They equated the millennium of Revelation 20 with the period of Church history from the time of Christ to the end of the world, or with a specific period of 1,000 years of that church history. They totally rejected the millenarianism or chiliasm of the early Fathers, Irenaeus and Justin for example, and found the militant chiliasm of the German Anabaptists deplorable. Yet Luther paved the way for the modification of eschatology by his historicist approach to the last book of the Bible, which he adopted in the second edition of his Notes on the New Testament. Henceforth most Protestant writers who commented on the Apocalypses of John and Daniel followed his lead and saw in their highly symbolic visions and dreams 'prophecies' of the downfall of the Turks, of the destruction of the city of Rome, of the demise of the Papacy, and of the ultimate triumph of the protestant Biblical religion. As it was widely believed that the end of the age was near these 'prophecies' seemed all the more relevant.
>
> The Augustinian historicist approach continued to be popular throughout the sixteenth and seventeenth centuries and amongst its more able exponents were John Bale, John Napier, and William Guild. But amongst some Calvinists it was modified by the inclusion of the doctrine (which was not explicitly taught by either St Augustine or Calvin) that near the end of the age large numbers of Jews, or perhaps the whole Jewish people, would be converted to Christianity from Judaism, and by their conversion bring great spiritual blessing to the Church on earth. This modified Augustinian historicist approach to eschatology probably owed its origin to the influence of Theodore Beza's Notes on the NT, in which he interpreted Romans 11:25ff, as meaning the future conversion of the Jewish people to Christ.[89]

The big takeaway here is that Beza introduced an historic hermeneutical mega-shift in understanding the term *Israel* in the NT as a referent to the Jewish people rather than to Christians. "He was followed by the vari-

---

[89] Toon, *Puritans, the Millennium, and the Future of Israel,* 6–7.

ous editors of the influential Geneva Bible. . . . In the 1557 and 1560 editions short notes explained that 'Israel' meant 'the nation of the Jews.' This development had an enormous impact on the thinking of Puritans in England, Scotland, and New England."[90] So the idea that God was not done with the Jewish people as in classic Supersessionism—that he still had plans for them—was no longer considered unthinkable.

A Future for the Land of Israel

"Historian Donald Lewis suggests that it was the Geneva Bible's vision of Israel's spiritual "return" or "turning" that prepared its huge readership for the associated idea of a literal return of Jews to their ancestral homeland."[91] Drawing from several sources, I have tried to list in chronological order the first writers to propose this return:

In 1585, Cambridge fellow Frances Kerr (1547–1589) called for the Jewish people to return to their land, but was later declared a heretic and burned at the stake.[92]

In 1588, Edmond Bunny (1540–1619), sub-dean of York cathedral, also proposed that the Jewish people would return to their native land.[93]

In 1608, Thomas Draxe (?–1618) did the same as well.

In 1611, Thomas Brightman's (1562–1607) posthumously published work on the book of Revelation, advocated the return of the Jewish people to the Holy Land: "There is nothing more sure: the Prophets plainly confirme [sic] it, and beat often upon it." His work laid the

---

90 Ibid., 24.

91 McDermott, *The New Christian Zionism*, 58; referencing Donald M. Lewis, *Origins of Christian Zionism: Lord Shaftesbury and Evangelical Support for a Jewish Homeland* (Cambridge: Cambridge University Press, 2010), 47.

92 Francis Kett, *The Glorious and Beautiful Garland of Mans Glorification Containing the Godly Misterie of Heavenly Jerusalem* (1585), in Stephen Spector, *Evangelicals and Israel: The Story of American Christian Zionism* (New York: Oxford University Press, 2009), 25; cited in Watson, *Dispensationalism Before Darby,* 15.

93 Edmond Bunny, *The Coronation of David* (1588) in Abba Hillel Silver, *The History of Messianic Speculation in Israel* (New York: Macmillan Co., 1927), 173; cited in Watson, *Dispensationalism Before Darby,* 15.

foundation for much future thought about eschatology and Israel, particularly by the Puritans.[94] William Watson provides a table listing 21 authors with the dates and titles of their books between the years 1584 and 1675 that were philo-Semitic.[95] It is interesting to note that this new, positive attitude towards the Jewish people fostered by these Protestant writers directly led to the readmission of the Jewish people back into England under Oliver Cromwell (c. 1655) after their expulsion 365 years earlier in 1290.

While the writers above—Kerr, Bunny, Draxe, and Brightman—are known only to scholars of the period, authors with greater name recognition also supported the idea of God's future plans for the Jewish people in their own land. Among them are John Cotton (1585–1652), the preeminent minister and theologian of the Massachusetts Bay Colony; John Bunyan (1628–1688), author of *The Pilgrim's Progress*; Increase Mather (1639–1723), pastor in Boston and President of Harvard College; and Jonathan Edwards (1703–1758), pastor, leader of revival, philosopher, and considered by many America's greatest theologian.[96]

The fact that such Christian "heavyweights" saw in Scripture the idea of the Jewish people returning to their land strengthened this theological view and made it much more difficult to dismiss as merely the product of the overwrought imaginations of a few obscure, eccentric clerics. On the other hand, the persuasive power of this emerging viewpoint was undermined by the fact that it was supported by a variety of speculations resulting from them that were quite varied.

For example:

- Some of the expositors were postmillennial in their understanding of eschatology, while others were premillennial.[97]

---

94 Thomas Brightman, *A Revelation of the Apocalyps* (Amsterdam: Hondius & Laurenss, 1611), 440; quoted in Robert O. Smith, *More Desired That Our Own Salvation: The Roots of Christian Zionism* (New York: Oxford University Press, 2013), 75; cited in McDermott, *The New Christian Zionism,* 59.

95 Watson, *Dispensationalism Before Darby,* 45.

96 McDermott, *The New Christian Zionism,* 61–65.

97 The millennium (L. *mille*–thousand + L. *annus*–year) or thousand years is mentioned six times in chapter 20 of the Book of Revelation. The prefixes often attached to it indicate in

- There were differences concerning whether the Jewish people *en masse* would become believers in Christ before they returned to the land or after.
- There were divergences of opinion as to whether the Jewish people would merely dwell in the land or once again become a geo-political unit, not to mention whether they would be first among the Nations.
- Some thought the recently discovered lands of the New World fit into biblical prophecy—one even positing the location of the New Jerusalem somewhere in Mexico.[98] Others thought not.
- Some thought the native inhabitants of the New World were the Ten Lost Tribes;[99] others, that they were the spawn of Satan.[100]
- There was also the vexing question as to whether the peoples on the earth in this future time would have natural bodies, resurrection bodies, or a combination of both!

In addition to this lack of consistency in viewpoints on God's future plans for Israel, for the most part they all suffered from a more funda-

---

systematic theologies when Christ will return in relation to the thousand years. Thus *pre*millennialism envisions Christ returning to earth *before* he reigns physically present on the earth for a thousand years; *post*millennialism sees the triumph of the gospel in such a way that the kingdom of God—God's reign through his people—is manifested on earth for either a literal or symbolic thousand years and then *after* it Christ returns, and; *a*millennialism postulates *no* millennium as described in the two previous scenarios but rather a "spiritual reign" of Christ and his followers for a symbolic thousand years which is coterminous with the period between Christ's Ascension and his return. See Craig A. Blaising, Kenneth L. Gentry Jr., and Robert B. Strimple, *Three Views of the Millennium and Beyond* (Grand Rapids, MI: Zondervan, 1999). For an older but still very helpful treatment and perhaps the "granddaddy" of "comparative views" works, see Robert G. Clouse, ed., *The Meaning of the Millennium: Four Views* (Downers Grove, IL: InterVarsity Press, 1977).

[98] Samuel Sewall, *Phaenomena quaedam Apocalyptica* (Boston, 1697); cited in Samuel Goldman, *God's Country: Christian Zionism in America* (Philadelphia, PA: U. of Penn. Press, 2018), 93.

[99] "Advancing a theory also promoted by the Puritan John Eliot, Menasseh [ben Israel, a Portuguese rabbi who wrote *The Hope of Israel*, 1650] suggested that the so-called Lost Tribes of Israel had made their way to the Americas, where they became the ancestors of the apparently indigenous peoples. . . . the Lost Tribes theory was [also] promoted by Thomas Thorowgood in his books [1650 & 1652]....[which] were widely circulated." Goldman, *God's Country*, 35.

[100] Increase Mather, *A Brief History of the Warr with the Indians in New England* (Boston: John Foster, 1676), 9; cited in Goldman, *God's Country*, 40.

mental problem. They basically left intact the narrative storyline of Supersessionism and simply "tacked on" a restoration of Israel to it. This approach gendered unanswered questions. Supersessionism posited simply that God used a *natural* Israel to bring forth the Messiah who would create a *spiritual* Israel—the church. Once that task was done, there was no more need for this special, natural Jewish people. To simply assert that the Tanakh prophesies a future natural kingdom for Israel and a few isolated NT verses seem to support it, doesn't show how such a future development fits into the overall narrative already established since the second century. It appears superfluous.

It seems a perennial truism across a variety of disciplines that the human mind is uncomfortable with ambiguity, let alone confusion and outright contradiction. It cries out for the cohesiveness of a *system*. That need was met by John Nelson Darby.

Darby's Dispensationalism

In his *Dispensationalism Before Darby*, William C. Watson goes to great lengths to demonstrate that, "The ideas expressed by Darby were present in earlier British theology dating back to English Puritanism..."[101] But he goes on to state that this occurred "long before Darby set them within a framework that subsequently arose as a *system* [my emphasis] in the 1800's,"[102] thus affirming Darby's unique systematizing role. Samuel Goldman puts it even more strongly:

> Darby did not invent any of these claims. The division of sacred history into eras, the emphasis on promises to Israel, and the insistence on the earthly nature of the millennium were recurring themes in Anglo-Protestant thought going back to the Reformation. The doctrine of the Rapture is more distinctive. Even so, it has precedents in the work of Increase Mather.[i] What was novel in premillennial dispensationalism was the way in which Darby made an *articulated system* [my empha-

---

101 Watson, *Dispensationalism Before Darby,* 2.
102 Ibid.

sis] of these elements."[103]

Clarence B. Bass summarizes the results of Darby's systematizing efforts: "The dispensationalist emphasis on the Jewish millennium, particularly with its teaching on the pre-tribulation rapture in order that the remnant of Israel may be gathered, all but replaced belief in historic premillennialism during the first part of this [20th] century."[104]

From the preceding we may gather that, until recently, Dispensationalism has been the ecclesiology and eschatology of choice for a large portion of those Christians who identify themselves as evangelical—and with it their concomitant support for the Jewish people and the State of Israel. Therefore, it behooves us to understand a little of the *who* behind it, *what* its main tenets are, *how* it ascended in popularity, and *why* it is now being massively abandoned.

The Who, What, How, & Why of Dispensationalism

Who: John Nelson Darby (1800–1882), known as the Father of Dispensationalism, was ordained in 1825 as a deacon of the established Church of Ireland. He enjoyed a brief, but fruitful ministry among the Irish Catholics, seeing hundreds come to the Lord. But that abruptly ended when William Magee, the Archbishop of Dublin, ruled that converts were obliged to swear allegiance to George IV as rightful king of Ireland.[105]

"He retired to a prayerful study of the position of the church in world affairs, and in 1829 published a pamphlet entitled *Considerations on*

---

103 Goldman, *God's Country,* 90. [i] Paul Boyer discusses Increase Mather's version of the Rapture in *When Time Shall Be No More* (Cambridge, MA: Belknap Press, 1994), 75.

104 Clarence B. Bass, *Backgrounds To Dispensationalism: Its Historic Genesis And Ecclesiastical Implications* (Grand Rapids, MI: Baker Book House, 1960), 146; citing C. Norman Krauss, *Dispensationalism in America* (Richmond, VA: John Knox Press, 1958), 104. "After tracing the conflict in the prophetic conferences of the late nineteenth century between the dispensational views and the historic premillennial view, Kraus concludes, '[By] 1901 ... the dispensationalists had won the day so completely that for the next fifty years friend and foe alike largely identified dispensationalism with premillennialism.'"

105 Ibid., 50–51.

the Nature and Unity of the Church of Christ, which has been called 'the [Plymouth] Brethren's first pamphlet.'"[106] Darby came to believe that the *kingdom* described in the Book of Isaiah and elsewhere in the Tanakh was entirely different from the Christian church. This radical distinction between the church and Israel became the key feature of the theological system he developed which came to be known as Dispensationalism.

What: The basic features of Dispensationalism have remained largely intact from its inception until today, with some modifications and clarifications added along the way. In *Dispensationalism*, Charles Ryrie[107] gives us a contemporary definition and description of the system:

> To summarize: Dispensationalism views the world as a household run by God. In His householdworld [sic] God is dispensing or administering its affairs according to His own will and in various stages of revelation in the passage of time. These various stages mark off the distinguishably different economies in the outworking of His total purpose, and these different economies constitute the dispensations. The understanding of God's differing economies is essential to a proper interpretation of His revelation within those various economies.[108]
>
> What marks off the various economies in the outworking of God's purpose and distinguishes each from the other? The answer is twofold: (1) the different governing relationship with the world into which God enters in each economy; and (2) the resulting responsibility on mankind in each of these different relationships.[109]
>
> The essence of dispensationalism is (1) the recognition of a consistent distinction between Israel and the church, (2) a consistent and regular use of a literal principle of interpretation, and (3) a basic and primary conception of the purpose of God as His own glory rather

---

106 Ibid.; citing W. Blair Neatby, *The History of the Plymouth Brethren* (London: Hodder & Stroughton, 1901), 18.

107 Charles C. Rylie, as a past president of Dallas Theological Seminary, author of the *Ryrie Study Bible* and the apologetic work *Dispensationalism Today* (1965) along with its updated and expanded version *Dispensationalism* (1995), is an outstanding representative of the Dispensational position.

108 Charles C. Ryrie, *Dispensationalism* (Chicago, IL: Moody Press, 1995), 24. Available as a pdf at http://shopeshop.org/Searchable%20Riches!/Authors/Ryrie,%20Charles/Dispensationalism.pdf (accessed June 25, 2018).

109 Ibid., 28.

than the salvation of mankind.[110]

There are the Dispensations of:[111]

1) Innocence (or freedom) – prior to Adam's fall
2) Conscience – Adam to Noah
3) Government – Noah to Abraham
4) Patriarchal rule (or promise) – Abraham to Moses
5) Mosaic Law – Moses to Christ
6) Grace – the current church age
7) Millennial Kingdom – Christ's return to Final Judgment → eternal state

How: Several factors help to explain how Dispensationalism became the dominant view among the majority of evangelicals throughout the English-speaking world and the mission fields they influenced. The following partial list is not meant to indicate an order of weight or influence:

- its prominence at prophecy conferences
- its exposition in the popular *Scofield Reference Bible*[112]
- its promotion by evangelist D. L. Moody and the institute and radio network named after him
- its emphasis on a "literal" interpretation of Scripture against the growing liberalism of the day[113]
- its approach to Scripture which strives to be systematic, complete, and coherent

---

[110] Ibid., 36.

[111] Ibid., 41–46.

[112] Since it appeared in 1909 [revised 1917], the *Scofield Reference Bible* has sold millions of copies and never been out of print. Its importance lay in the notes and cross-references that Scofield, a participant in the prophecy conferences, interspersed with the biblical text in a manner reminiscent of the Geneva edition of the sixteenth century. Goldman, *God's Country,* 148.

[113] Liberalism or Modernism attempted to keep Christianity "relevant" to contemporary culture by moving away from the classical view of the inspiration of Scripture and the Reformation's grammatical-historical approach to interpreting it in favor of viewing Scripture as merely the product of human reflections on the divine—full of allegories, symbols, and myths. Dispensationalism, with its emphasis on the plain meaning of Scripture—specifically, Israel always means Israel, never the church—by contrast was promoted to be the only system around that was upholding "the faith once for all delivered to the saints" (Jude 3)!

- its packaging in the mass appeal formats of *The Late Great Planet Earth*[114] and the *Left Behind*[115] series
- its support of Israel and the Jewish people[116]
- its appeal to the perennially fascinating subject of what the future holds

Why: Despite the popularity of the relatively recent *Left Behind* series mentioned previously, over the past three decades, Dispensationalism has been on the decline among evangelicals. The following is a partial list of reasons why this is occurring, and again, is not meant to indicate any particular order of weight or influence:

- Tends to be associated with "fundamentalism" and perceived as a less sophisticated approach to biblical hermeneutics
- Exhaustion/embarrassment over "end-times" signs and predictions that have not come to pass
- Jesus clearly taught about *something* of the reality of the kingdom of God being for *right now* as well as it being something to come in the future (commonly referred to as the "already/not yet" of the kingdom, or *inauguration/consummation*).[117] Contrariwise, Dispensationalism teaches that the church has nothing to do with the *postponed* kingdom.
- Along with the last point above and the concept of the any moment rapture of the church, this leaves the church with no mandate to

---

[114] Hal Lindsay, *The Late Great Planet Earth* (Grand Rapids, MI: Zondervan, 1970). The New York Times called it the "no. 1 non-fiction bestseller of the decade" (from the back cover). It was the first book on biblical prophecy that anyone of the baby boomer generation who came to Christ during The Jesus Movement read.

[115] The *Left Behind* series consists of 16 novels written by Tim LaHaye and Jerry B. Jenkins between 1995 and 2007, covering all aspects of the Dispensational end-times scenario. Four of them were made into movies.

[116] The facts of Israel becoming a nation in 1948 and the reuniting of the city of Jerusalem in 1967 seemed to confirm the prophetic program of Dispensationalism; not to mention the appeal of its philosemitic stance in the wake of the Holocaust.

[117] The *already/not-yet* dynamic has now been recognized by most NT exegetes—both Reformed and not-Reformed, Protestant and Catholic. For example, see George E. Ladd, *The Gospel of the Kingdom: Popular Expositions on the Kingdom of God* (Grand Rapids, MI: Eerdmans Publishing Co., 1959.

be a force for good in the world. In fact, C. I. Schofield in his reference Bible states that each dispensation "ends in judgment—marking his [man's] utter failure in every dispensation"[118] and thus the church will necessarily fail in her Great Commission task.

- Its tight compartmentalization of the different ways God deals with humans in each dispensation and specifically its total separation between anything to do with the church and anything to do with Israel[119] leads to many arcane, convoluted interpretations of Scripture. As just one example, many Christians would be surprised to learn that the Lord's prayer, "Our Father…Thy kingdom come" is not to be prayed by "church age" saints. They are to be looking for the any moment coming of Jesus—not the kingdom. Thus, this prayer will be prayed by those who are "left behind" after the rapture of the church during the Tribulation period![120] Samuel P. Tregelles, noted biblical scholar, textual critic, and one of the early Plymouth Brethren, in rejecting Darby's new interpretation termed it the "height of speculative nonsense."[121]

Dispensing with Dispensationalism

Dispensationalism currently represents the only *well-known*, *systematic* (please note these qualifiers) theology that recognizes a place for the Jewish people and their ancient homeland in the economy of God. As some Christians abandon it, they tend to go back to the only other *systematic* theology on this issue available, i.e., classic Supersessionism. This is unfortunate because this gets them heading in the wrong direction. As Karl Barth observed, Dispensationalism's errors were "errors in the

---

118 C. I. Schofield, *Schofield Reference Bible* (Oxford University Press, 1917 edition), p. 5 ftnt. 4; cited in Bass, *Backgrounds To Dispensationalism,* 19.

119 "Comparing then, what is said in Scripture concerning Israel and the Church, we find that in origin, calling, promise, worship, principles of conduct and future destiny all is contrast." C. I. Schofield, *Schofield Correspondence Course* (Chicago, IL: Moody Bible Institute, 19th edition, 22–25; cited in Bass, *Backgrounds to Dispensationalism,* 28.

120 George D. Beckwith, *God's Prophetic Plan* (Grand Rapids, MI: Zondervan, 1942) 98ff; cited in Bass, *Backgrounds to Dispensationalism,* 42.

121 Samuel P. Tregelles as quoted in Charles E. Brown, *The Reign of Christ* (Anderson, IN: Gospel Trumpet, Co., 1950), 4. cited in Bass, *Backgrounds to Dispensationalism,* 21.

right direction."[122]

This classic Supersessionism making a strong comeback in certain evangelical circles is often coupled with a strong "social justice" message (read "poor, oppressed Palestinians against big, bad Israel") that appeals particularly to the young. Though unwittingly, this position plays into the hands of the secular far Left and Islamic extremists who would like to completely delegitimize the modern state of Israel by resuscitating old anti-Jewish/antisemitic stereotypes and tropes. Fortunately, a growing number of evangelicals are turning to an option that sees a central role for the Jewish people in the purposes of God in a way that is more biblically integrated than either Dispensationalism or Supersessionism.

---

122 Carys Moseley, *Nationhood, Providence, and Witness: Israel in Protestant Theology and Social Theory* (Eugene, OR: Cascade, 2013), xx; in Gerald McDermott, ed., *The New Christian Zionism,* 72.

FIVE

BEGIN WITH THE END IN MIND: "ISRAEL AND THE NATIONS"

In the previous two chapters we saw that historically the church dealt with the mystery of Israel by positing only two *systemic* responses—Supersessionism and Dispensationalism. Each had something to commend it or faithful, Bible-believing Christians would not have subscribed to either of them. On the other hand, it is clear from the history of biblical interpretation that each was lacking in significant ways. Robert Saucy highlights this point and suggests a way forward:

> In our opinion there is a mediating position between non-dispensationalism and traditional dispensationalism that provides a better understanding of Scripture. This view seeks to retain a natural understanding of the prophetic Scriptures that appear to assign a significant role to the nation Israel in the future, in accordance with a dispensational system. But it also sees the program of God as unified *within* history, in agreement with non-dispensationalists, and it denies a radical discontinuity between the present church age and the messianic kingdom promises....
>
> In our understanding of biblical history, then, Scripture teaches a "unity with distinctives," fusing together what might be termed the primary emphases of both dispensational and non-dispensational theology. Although traditional dispensationalism, as we see it, has tended to draw distinctives too sharply, it must be credited with calling attention to the particularities of biblical history that were ignored and vir-

> tually eliminated in other theological systems. By contrast, non-dispensational scholars have encouraged us to focus on the truth of the unity of God's historical work.[123]

The contemporary church does not have recourse to universal councils to clarify and resolve doctrinal controversies. However, one can hope that the proliferation of scholarly focus on this subject and the rapid and broad dissemination of those efforts will result in an emergent, widely shared consensus on how to talk about the mystery of Israel in a more biblically consistent way.

BEGIN WITH THE END IN MIND

Stephen Covey, in his insightful *Seven Habits of Highly Effective People*, identifies Habit Two as "Begin with the End in Mind."[124] Indeed, "from Plato to Hegel and beyond, some of the greatest philosophers declared that what you think about death, and life beyond it, is the key to thinking seriously about everything else—and, indeed, that it provides one of the main reasons for thinking seriously about anything at all. This is something a Christian theologian should heartily endorse."[125] As I was talking with my wife Sylvia about our need to do this as we grapple with trying to understand the overarching plan of God as it is revealed in the Scriptures, she stated the obvious, but I fear all-too-often overlooked truism that, "*God* begins with the end in mind," e.g., "I am God, and there is no other; I am God, and there is none like me, declaring the end

---

123 Robert L. Saucy, *The Case for Progressive Dispensationalism: The Interface Between Dispensational and Non-Dispensational Theology* (Grand Rapids, MI: Zondervan Publishing House, 1993), 27, 29. The very appearance of newly minted constructs such as Progressive Dispensationalism and Progressive Covenantalism* lends strong support to the thesis that the church has neglected the mystery of Israel and has historically, until now, offered only two very inadequate systems of thought about the subject. * See Stephen J. Wellum and Brent E. Parker, eds., *Progressive Covenantalism: Charting a Course between Dispensational and Covenantal Theologies* (Nashville, TN: B & H Academic, 2016).

124 Stephen R. Covey, *Seven Habit of Highly Effective People: Powerful Lessons in Personal Change* (New York, NY: Free Press, a div. of Simon & Shuster, Inc., 1989), 95–144.

125 N. T. Wright, *Surprised By Hope: Rethinking Heaven, the Resurrection, & the Mission of the Church* (New York, NY: Harper One, 2008), 6.

from the beginning and from ancient times things not yet done, saying, 'My counsel shall stand, and I will accomplish all my purpose'" (Isa. 46:9b–10).

Thinking about the end God has in mind for the earth can perhaps help us understand how we are going to get there, i.e., guide us in discerning the overarching narrative and trajectory of Scripture. Now it is true that David humbly declared, "O LORD, my heart is not lifted up; my eyes are not raised too high; I do not occupy myself with things too great and too marvelous for me" (Ps. 131:1); and Paul cautioned "For now we see in a mirror dimly … Now I know in part" (1 Cor. 13:12); while Yogi Berra observed "It's tough to make predictions, especially about the future" (his wit). Nevertheless, armed with these appropriate caveats, one who takes the Bible seriously must acknowledge that God has given to us in both the Tanakh and the NT, at least in broad outlines, what he has in store for planet earth.

HEAVEN: IT'S NOT THE END OF THE WORLD

The title of David Lawrence's 1995 book wonderfully summarizes the biblical concept I want to convey in this section—*Heaven: It's Not the End of the World! The Biblical Promise of a New Earth.*[126] The main idea he conveys, that the believer's ultimate destiny is the new earth (with heaven intimately joined to it), is not radical speculation, but rather a thoroughly biblical construct of the future held by many theologians in the history of the church.

So I must confess that I was quite surprised when I began to share this concept with a dear friend and Christian leader that he was *shocked* at the idea. Furthermore, when I preached on these matters a few years ago in my church, I got a similar reaction. Forget for a moment any talk about the mystery of Israel in the plan of God; apparently just talking about his future plans for planet earth generally can cause "shock and

---

126 David Lawrence, *Heaven: It's Not the End of the World! The Biblical Promise of a New Earth* (London: Scripture Union, 1995).

awe" in those who have been led to believe that the *current* heaven is the end for the believer. And in all fairness, if you think about some of the hymns which have nurtured them in their Christian faith, it is no wonder:

> "Some glad morning, when this life is over, I'll fly away / to a home where joy will never end, I'll fly away"; "This world is not my home, I'm just a-passing through / my treasures are laid up, somewhere beyond the blue"; "When the trumpet of the Lord shall sound and time will be no more; when the morning breaks eternal bright and fair / When His chosen ones are gathered to Him on the other shore, and the roll is called up yonder I'll be there"; "When we all get to heaven, what a day of rejoicing that will be / When we all see Jesus, we'll sing and shout the victory."

Please, please, do not think for a moment that I cite these beloved songs in order to be derogatory or to make a mockery of them. On the contrary, they are beautiful expressions of biblical truth or they wouldn't have endured and brought so much comfort to faithful believers over the years. They are true—but incomplete. When one who trusts in Jesus dies, that one will immediately be with the Lord (2 Cor. 5:8; Phil. 1:22–24). And since the Lord Jesus is currently in the realm called *heaven*, that is where that believer will be. But the believer will not remain in that "intermediate" state. There is something even greater coming—the resurrection of the body in order to live in a new world, a new earth.

I'm afraid the same incompleteness highlights the appeals in much of our preaching: "If you died tonight, do you know where you would go? Do you know for sure you would go to heaven?" Again, if we understand the use of the word *heaven* as metonymy (the substitution of the name of an attribute or adjunct for that of the thing meant, for example *suit* for *business executive*, or *the track* for *horse racing*),[127] then the appeal is completely true and legitimate. But after much repetition and little or no

---

[127] Oxford University Press, "Metonymy," https://en.oxforddictionaries.com/definition/metonymy (accessed July 13, 2018).

follow through, the "thing meant"—resurrection and dwelling on a new earth—has gotten lost.

The subtitle of N. T. Wright's book *Surprised by Hope: Rethinking Heaven, the Resurrection, & the Mission of the Church,* supplies a pithy summary of what the church needs to do and is beginning to do in this hour. The following excerpts from it get to the heart of the matter:

> A massive assumption has been made in Western Christianity that the purpose of being a Christian is simply, or at least mainly, to "go to heaven when you die," and texts that don't say that but that mention heaven are read as if they did say it, and texts that say the opposite, like Romans 8:18–25 and Revelation 21–22, are simply screened out as if they didn't exist. . . . [The early Christians] believed that God was going to do for the whole cosmos what he had done for Jesus at Easter. . . . To put it bluntly, creation is to be redeemed; that is, space is to be redeemed, time is to be redeemed, and matter is to be redeemed. God said "very good" over his space-time-and-matter creation, and though the redeeming of this world from its present corruption and decay will mean transformations we cannot imagine, the one thing we can be sure of is that this redeeming of creation will not mean that God will say, of space, time and matter, "Oh, well, nice try, good while it lasted but obviously gone bad, so let's drop it and go for a nonspatiotemporal, nonmaterial world instead. But if God really does intend to redeem rather than to reject his created world of space, time, and matter, we are faced with the question: what might it look like to celebrate that redemption, that healing and transformation, in the present, and thereby appropriately to anticipate God's final intention?"[128]

Robert Saucy also highlights the problem of theologically juxtaposing or contrasting the material and the "spiritual":

> Some scholars conclude that with the coming of the spiritual realities of Christ and the Spirit, the physical, or material, loses its meaning. Thus Christ becomes the real meaning of the land or the temple or even Israel. According to this reasoning, the coming of the spiritual

[128] Wright, *Surprised by Hope,* 93; 90; 211–212.

> realities somehow requires eliminating the physical or material dimension of things. But the idea that a move away from the material to the spiritual is a genuine advancement in salvation history sounds suspiciously Platonic.
>
> By contrast, the Old Testament prophets saw no problem with the physical and material existing together with the spiritual in eschatological times—analogous to the original creation, which included the material. For those prophets, the outpouring of the Spirit and even his indwelling in the human heart could exist alongside the material realities of Israel's restoration to the land, the city of Jerusalem, and the temple. Although the new spiritual realities brought changes—especially in the direct relationship of God, through the Spirit, with all people everywhere—these changes apparently did not rule out the reality and significance of the physical in God's eschatological plan.[129]

Followers of Jesus have always believed that he rose again bodily—that is the very definition of resurrection. In *The Apostles' Creed* they confessed that they, too, would participate in a future resurrection: "I believe ... in the resurrection of the body."[130] In the same Creed they also confessed that "he will come again." Christ came, the first time, to earth. When we confess that he will come *again*, the idea is that he will come again *to earth*. We get this from such unequivocal passages as Acts 1:11, where Jesus's apostles were instructed by angels following his ascension into the heavens, "Men of Galilee, why do you stand looking into heaven? This Jesus, who was taken up from you into heaven, will come in the same way as you saw him go into heaven." We don't need resurrection bodies if all we are going to do is inhabit some ethereal, non-material realm. But if according to the promises we going to be reigning with Jesus, and Jesus is reigning on the earth in his resurrection body, then we also will be on the earth in resurrection bodies celebrating the goodness of God's new creation.

---

129 Saucy, *The Case for Progressive Dispensationalism,* 30–31.

130 Walter A. Elwell, ed., "Apostles' Creed," in *The Evangelical Dictionary of Theology*, 72. This belief comes directly from the Jewish people and the Tanakh. (See John D. Levenson, *Resurrection and the Restoration of Israel: The Ultimate Victory of the God of Life* (New Haven, CT: Yale University Press, 2006).

Just to be clear on where I am going with this line of argumentation, Russel Moore reminds us:

> Augustine, perhaps the most influential theologian of the early church, systematized what theologian Craig Blaising calls a "spiritual vision" model of eschatology as opposed to a "new creation" model of a restored earth and continuity between bodily life now and in the eschaton. For Augustine, the hope of the Christian was not earthly but heavenly. He held to a resurrection of the body but described heaven in term of the beatific vision.[131]

Randy Alcorn, in his magisterial book *Heaven*,[132] sets forth the most comprehensive treatment of this subject ever attempted. I have culled a few supporting quotes from the many throughout his book by different authors, past and present, who support the view of God redeeming and restoring his original creation with resurrected humans living on the earth. I have listed them in the Appendix for further reference.

The fact that many theologians agree upon a subject does not mean that they are correct. However, it should give us pause to reconsider how we may have popularly understood the Christian view of the afterlife. Earlier theologians did not write extensively about the subject; contemporary theologians are. The emerging picture is that there is going to come a "time for restoring[133] all the things about which God spoke by the mouth of his holy prophets long ago" (Acts 3:21). And central to the "all the things" to be restored of which the prophets spoke repeatedly are the Nations—and Israel.

---

131 Russel D. Moore, "The Doctrine of Last Things" in *A Theology for the Church,* ed. Daniel L. Akin (Nashville, TN: H & B Publishing Group, 2007), 871.

132 Randy Alcorn, *Heaven* (Carol Stream, IL: Tyndale House Publishers, 2004).

133 "The word Peter uses for 'restoration' is the same word *(apokatastasis)* used in the Septuagint (which the early church used as its Bible) for God's future return of Jews from all over the world to Israel." E.g., Jer. 16:16: 'I will bring them back *[apokatastēsō]* to their own land that I gave to their fathers.' Apparently Peter did not think that the return of the Babylonian exiles at the end of the sixth century BC fulfilled all the prophecies of a future worldwide return to the land. McDermott, *The New Christian Zionism*, 54.

ISRAEL AND THE NATIONS

Happily, "many contemporary theologians decry disembodied eschatologies of yesterday by teaching the new heavens and new earth to come."[134] However, "they typically strip the new earth of the distinctive nationalities and the centrally placed nation [Israel] as depicted in the Bible. It is akin to giving the resurrected body of an individual a nondistinctive face so that it could not be distinguished from the myriads of other faces in the world to come."[135]

Gerald McDermott identifies this key theological failure as one of not appreciating both the universal and the particular dimensions of God's good creation and restoration of it:

> Most systematic theology today, when it treats Israel, betrays a modernist bent. As Peter Ochs suggests, anti-Zionist theology flies with one wing.* It tries to fly with the wing of universalism but without the corresponding wing of particularity. This was the hallmark of modernity, starting with Lessing's "ugly, great ditch" between universal reason and the particulars of history that he and most Enlightenment thinkers after him thought could not be jumped.** Hence, despite the fact that God made clear in his First Testament that he saves the world (the universal) through the particular (Israel), much of Christian theology today treats the Second (New) Testament as if it also rejects the diversity of the particular for the homogeneity of the universal. No longer is Jew different from Gentile in most Christian theologies; nor is the land of Israel of any significance—even though, as this book has shown, the New Testament authors held the land and people of Israel to be of future significance. The result is a strange universality in eschatology, where there is no interrelationship among different peoples or nations in the eschaton. Instead, there is the dominance of eternal abstractions—submission to a non-Jewish deity by myriads of human beings without national or ethnic distinctions. This is Gnostic and Docetic eschatology, in which matter is absent (Gnostic) or blandly undifferentiated and therefore only *seemingly* important (Docetic). All

---

[134] Ibid., 325.
[135] Ibid., 325.

these eschatologies have a kind of geometric beauty, perhaps, but they lack the nonsymmetrical beauty of biblical eschatology.[136]

In sum, a growing minority of scholarly voices are calling us to take seriously, not only the redemption/restoration of the *all* of God's original good creation in both its "material" and "spiritual" dimensions (the universal), but also the *distinctives* within that creation (the particulars). It is abundantly clear from both the Tanakh and the NT that in the end we find, not just a homogenized, non-differentiated conglomerate called humanity, but distinct Nations, nationalities, complete with all of the artful variations on the human theme that our creative God intended. And Israel, far from being excluded from this picture, is in the center of it.

For the sake of space, I am going to take the risk that the reader will grant the premise that the Tanakh clearly depicts Israel as a nation in the midst of the Nations in the future age.[137] Below I have listed just a few passages from the NT which depict "Israel and the Nations" "still in play" at the end of this age and moving into eternity:

> "Behold, your house is left to you desolate; and I say to you, you will not see Me until the time comes when you say, 'BLESSED IS HE WHO COMES IN THE NAME OF THE LORD!'" (Luke 13:35)[138]

Jesus, in his lament over Jerusalem, cites Psalm 118:26 and indicates that

---

136 Ibid., 324–325. *Peter Ochs, *Another Reformation: Postliberal Christianity and the Jews* (Grand Rapids, MI: Baker Academic, 2011), 28; ** Gotthold Ephraim Lessing, "On the Proof of Spirit and Power," in *Lessing's Theological Writings,* ed. and trans. Henry Chadwick (Redwood City, CA: Stanford University Press, 1957), 51–56.

137 We see a new or renewed earth (Isaiah 66:22). We see Nature transformed (Isaiah 11:6–9). We see a resurrected (Daniel 12:2) Jewish people dwelling in shalom with the nations (Isaiah 2:4). All are worshiping the one true God—which is the God of Abraham, Isaac, and Jacob (Isaiah 2:3; 66:23). Much more could be said and many more verses cited, but this is enough to highlight the fact that at the end of time, the *Tanakh* depicts "Israel and the Nations" living in peace on a renewed earth.

138 I used the NASB version here because of its custom of highlighting portions from the Tanakh cited in the NT in ALL CAPS. *New American Standard Bible,* Copyright © 1960, 1962, 1963, 1968, 1971, 1972, 1973, 1975, 1977, 1995 by The Lockman Foundation and used by permission.

"the time" is coming in the future when the Jewish people of Jerusalem will welcome him. When we remember that *Jerusalem* in Scripture often stands in synecdoche for all of Israel (as we say Washington, London, or Paris to refer to their respective countries) and that her chief governing body the Sanhedrin is located there, it further strengthens the idea of a corporate future for the Jewish people—and that it occurs in the land!

> They will fall by the edge of the sword and be led captive among all nations, and Jerusalem will be trampled underfoot by the Gentiles, until the times of the Gentiles are fulfilled. (Luke 21:24)

As the context makes unequivocally clear, Jesus is speaking about the Jewish people and foretelling what is going to happen to them.[139] Furthermore, he predicts that the Gentiles (non-Jewish peoples) would have control of Jerusalem *until the times of the Gentiles are fulfilled.* This phrase can only mean that at some future point, Jerusalem is not controlled by the Gentiles. So if it is not controlled by them at this future time, who is in control of it? Well, unless we want to posit that Jerusalem will be wiped out of existence or lie in uninhabited desolation—neither of which options are supported by the Tanakh or the NT—then it must come under control of the only other people who are not included in the category *Gentile,* i.e., the Jewish people.

> Now if their trespass means riches for the world, and if their failure means riches for the Gentiles, how much more will their fullness[140] mean! . . . For if their rejection means the reconciliation of the world, what will their acceptance mean but life from the dead? . . . As regards the gospel, they are enemies for your sake. But as regards election,

139 Conservative scholarship dates the writing of the *Gospel According to Luke* to sometime before the destruction of the temple in 70. But even if one sides with liberal scholarship and puts it in the 80's, it still does not explain Jesus's uncanny prediction that the Jewish people would be led away to all the nations. That simply had not yet happened.

140 The ESV version which I am using throughout this book has "full inclusion." This is not necessarily a wrong inference, but it is an inference, not a translation. The footnote says "Lit. *their fullness*" which I used here and which is in agreement with most other translations of this passage.

> they are beloved for the sake of their forefathers. For the gifts and the calling of God are irrevocable. (Rom. 11:12, 15, 28-29)

Observe (as Theodore Beza did four and a half centuries ago and the majority of commentators today) that at the end of the age Israel/ethnically Jewish people will respond en masse to their God's Messianic call. Notice further, that the gifts they have received and their calling in the plan of God have never been revoked.[141]

> Then I saw another angel ascending from the rising of the sun, with the seal of the living God, and he called with a loud voice to the four angels who had been given power to harm earth and sea, saying, "Do not harm the earth or the sea or the trees, until we have sealed the servants of our God on their foreheads." And I heard the number of the sealed, 144,000, sealed from every tribe of the sons of Israel:
> 12,000 from the tribe of Judah were sealed,
> 12,000 from the tribe of Reuben,
> 12,000 from the tribe of Gad,
> 12,000 from the tribe of Asher,
> 12,000 from the tribe of Naphtali,
> 12,000 from the tribe of Manasseh,
> 12,000 from the tribe of Simeon,
> 12,000 from the tribe of Levi,
> 12,000 from the tribe of Issachar,
> 12,000 from the tribe of Zebulun,
> 12,000 from the tribe of Joseph,
> 12,000 from the tribe of Benjamin were sealed.
> After this I looked, and behold, a great multitude that no one could

[141] In Rom. 9:4–5 Paul give a list of eight privileges which "...currently 'belongs' to 'Israelites.' It is not that they once belonged to Israel or have been transferred to another. Israel still possesses them, even while in unbelief.... Paul's mention of 'covenants' and 'promises' raises the issue of their content. Since he offers no qualifications, all dimensions of the covenants and promises as explained in the prophets are probably in view. No indication exists that only salvation blessings are intended or that physical and national aspects have been spiritualized or made into something else. In Gal. 3:15 Paul says that once a covenant is ratified, 'no one sets it aside or adds conditions to it.' So the spiritual, physical, and national components of God's promises as originally revealed are significant because of God's character." Michael J. Vlach, "A Non-Typological Future-Mass-Conversion View," in *Three Views of Israel and the Church,* eds. Compton and Naselli, 67.

> number, from every nation, from all tribes and peoples and languages, standing before the throne and before the Lamb, clothed in white robes, with palm branches in their hands, and crying out with a loud voice, "Salvation belongs to our God who sits on the throne, and to the Lamb!" (Rev. 7:2-10)

Here we are in the last book of the Bible (pretty late in the ballgame) and we see not only Israel, but Israel listed specifically by tribes. While I understand that the book of Revelation is an apocalyptic literature, that it is full of symbols, and that it can be difficult to interpret in certain of its particulars, it still seems a stretch to deny that this portion of Scripture refers to ethnically Jewish people. We have already seen that in the history of theology that the hermeneutic of equating the terms *church* and *Israel* is on very shaky ground at best. To then extrapolate and say, "Well, since the church is Israel it must also be represented by the twelve tribes" is a bridge too far. Nowhere else in the NT is the church equated with the twelve tribes. Contrariwise, the four instances outside of Revelation (Matt. 19:28; Luke 22:30; Acts 26:7; Jas. 1:1) where the phrase *twelve tribes* appears in the NT clearly refer to ethnically Jewish people. When we see this group of twelve tribes mentioned in conjunction with the Nations, it is more appropriate to understand this passage as another reinforcement of the theme of "Israel and the Nations." By the way, notice also that the *Nations*, although as a group are distinct from Israel, are nonetheless not an undifferentiated mass of humanity, but are also distinct peoples from each other—"from every nation, from all tribes and peoples and languages."

> Then I saw a new heaven and a new earth, for the first heaven and the first earth had passed away, and the sea was no more. And I saw the holy city, new Jerusalem, coming down out of heaven from God, prepared as a bride adorned for her husband. . . . Then came one of the seven angels who had the seven bowls full of the seven last plagues and spoke to me, saying, "Come, I will show you the Bride, the wife of the Lamb." And he carried me away in the Spirit to a great, high mountain, and showed me the holy city Jerusalem coming down out

> of heaven from God, having the glory of God, its radiance like a most rare jewel, like a jasper, clear as crystal. It had a great, high wall, with twelve gates, and at the gates twelve angels, and on the gates the names of the twelve tribes of the sons of Israel were inscribed—on the east three gates, on the north three gates, on the south three gates, and on the west three gates. And the wall of the city had twelve foundations, and on them were the twelve names of the twelve apostles of the Lamb. . . . By its light will the nations walk, and the kings of the earth will bring their glory into it, and its gates will never be shut by day—and there will be no night there. They will bring into it the glory and the honor of the nations. (Rev. 21:1–2, 9–14, 24–26)

Here the setting is not "late in the ball game"—the "ball game" is over! We have now moved into eternity as we see a new heaven and a new earth depicted as was also promised in the Tanakh (Isa. 65:17; 66:22). In describing this new earth we find again the use of the phrase *twelve tribes* along with the descriptor *of the sons of Israel.* Notice also how their names are mentioned in close proximity to *the names of the twelve apostles of the lamb.* This could perhaps be related to Jesus' statement to his apostles, "Jesus said to them, 'Truly, I say to you, in the new world (Gk. παλιγγενεσίᾳ - *regeneration*), when the Son of Man will sit on his glorious throne, you who have followed me will also sit on twelve thrones, judging the twelve tribes of Israel.'" (Matt. 19:28; see also Lk. 22:28–30).[142] Furthermore, we see the Nations with rulers over them. Again, we do not have a mere undifferentiated, conglomeration of people called humanity. Rather, we see "Israel and the Nations." Some object that talk of a future for a people called Israel in a land called Israel is to abandon that which is *spiritual* and to revert to that which is *carnal.* But it is not *carnal*, it is *creational!*[143]

---

[142] A number of commentators understand this *judging* to refer to leading or ruling as those designated as judges did in the book of Judges. See McDermott, *The New Christian Zionism,* 137–138.

[143] But for virtually all of them [first generation Protestant Reformers] the hope of the church was essentially spiritual, heavenly, and amillennial. In keeping with the church fathers, the Magisterial Reformers identified Israel with the "spiritual Israel," the church … Calvin and Luther particularly denounced the idea of a physical, material, historical manifestation of the kingdom of God to be "carnal" and "Jewish"—unfit for a Christian understanding of a spir-

A Hermeneutical Hook

It is significant that we see "Israel and the Nations" depicted as continuing into eternity for at least two reasons. First, it is in harmony with and reinforces the consistent theme of Scripture that "God has never given up on his original creation. Yet we've somehow managed to overlook an entire biblical vocabulary that makes this point clear. *Reconcile. Redeem. Restore. Recover. Return. Renew. Regenerate. Resurrect.* Each of these biblical words begins with the *re-* prefix, suggesting a return to an original condition that was ruined or lost. (Many are translations of Greek words with an *ana-* prefix, which has the same meaning as the English re-.)"[144] That which is true of every aspect of God's very good creation he is also going to do for the Nations which he created.

The second reason this is significant is that it provides us with a "hermeneutical hook" to guide us in understanding how we should read passages about them that we find earlier in the biblical story. As "we begin with the end in mind," we find "Israel and the Nations" at the end of the story, so we shouldn't read any texts in such a way that might imply that God will ultimately be done with them. Rather, since we see "Israel and the Nations" relating to each other in the NT—all the way to the end—then we should be watching for how they relate and interplay in the earlier portions of Scripture. The old preachers used to assert that there is a "scarlet thread" (think of Rahab in Josh 2 and 6) of blood running through the Scriptures—emphasizing the theme of sacrifice.[145] In a similar way, if our eyes are opened to it, we can see the thread of God's purposes for "Israel and the Nations" running through the whole Bible. That's what the following chapters are all about.

---

itual kingdom. Russel D. Moore, "The Doctrine of Last Things" in *A Theology for the Church*, ed. Daniel L. Akin (Nashville, TN: H & B Publishing Group, 2007), 871.

144 Randy Alcorn, *Heaven*, 88.

145 See, for example, W. A. Criswell, *The Scarlett Thread Through The Bible* (Nashville, TN: Lifeway Press, 2014) which also available as a pdf at http://storage.cloversites.com/firstchurchofchrist1/documents/The%20Scarlet%20Thread.pdf (accessed December 5, 2018). A Google search for *scarlet thread through the Bible* will yield the titles of several other books on this theme.

SIX

GETTING THE BIG STORY RIGHT

The subtitle of the first chapter in *The New Christian Zionism* highlights a major challenge to all of us when reading the Bible: "Getting the Big Story Wrong." The editor of the book and author of this first chapter Gerald McDermott elaborates:

> The Bible is extraordinarily complex. While the sixteenth-century Protestant Reformers rightly insisted that its basic message of salvation could be understood by the simplest of sinners, they also believed that its preachers needed extensive training to be able to understand its many subtleties and profundities. They also knew that it is impossible to interpret the Bible rightly without having the right framework or lens through which to read it. The little stories could not be understood without knowing the Big Story into which they fit. Using the wrong Big Story would cause Christians to misinterpret the hundreds of little stories in the Bible, not to mention the meaning of the myriads of details from ancient cultures in ancient times.
>
> For this reason it is essential that we get the big picture right. As I mentioned at the beginning of the introduction, the New Christian Zionism insists that the story of Israel is central to the story of salvation. The latter is fundamentally misunderstood and distorted when it omits Israel and her story with God. The sheer size of the Hebrew Scriptures, which dwarf the New Testament, should have signaled this to the historic church. But so does the gospel story in the New Tes-

tament, which portrays Israel at the center.[146]

All informed students of the Bible would agree to McDermott's first proposition: "it is essential that we get the big picture right." However, some might very well balk is at his second proposition: "Israel is central to the story of salvation." They might say, "Wait a minute! Isn't *Jesus* supposed to be the center of the salvation story?" On its face, it is a fair question. But I believe upon deeper reflection we will see that it sets up a false dichotomy. What is "the salvation story"? The Chalcedonian Creed (451) says the purpose of the incarnation was "for us and for our salvation." If there is no "us" in desperate need "salvation," then there is no need for the incarnation. So while we can say that the Bible is certainly and ultimately about God revealing himself for his glory, it does so by telling the story of his creation gone awry "us" and what he is doing about it "for our salvation." That "us" contains "Israel and the Nations" and the "for our salvation" contains his calling of Israel to demonstrate to the Nations who he is, what his character is like, and who his rightful Messiah will be as opposed to false messiahs that will come to deceive. Thus, it is not incorrect to observe that "Israel is central to the story of salvation."

Confession or Omission of Faith?

Several years ago, I led our congregation through a series of messages on *The Apostles' Creed.*[147] While this creed has served the church well for centuries, it has some glaring omissions which the commentators[148] on it whom I consulted faithfully highlighted—even though they cherished the document. There is a simple reason for this. While the Creed was used as a summary confession of the Christian understanding of God

146 McDermott, *The New Christian Zionism,* 33.

147 See footnote in "Introduction" in the subsection **The Structure.**

148 Luke Timothy Johnson, *The Creed: What Christians Believe and Why It Matters* (New York, NY: Doubleday, 2005); Alister McGrath, *I Believe: Exploring The Apostles' Creed* (Downers Grove, IL: IVP Books, 1991, 1997); J. I. Packer, *Affirming the Apostles' Creed* (Wheaton, IL: Crossway, 2008).

and his purposes in Jesus, it was crafted in response to certain concerns. So as J. I. Packer points out:

> We should note as background that in the second century, when the Creed was crystallizing throughout the Christian world, the church was constantly harassed by sheep-stealing Gnostics. Their very name made an elitist boast; to catch the proud nuance of the Greek word *gnōstikoi,* you need to render it as "those in the know." And their Gnosticism was in fact an imaginative intellectualism that claimed to give the "real meaning" of each Christian doctrine, something that (so the Gnostics said) Christians regularly miss by reason of their mistaken idea that spirit and matter can interact to the point of uniting, and indeed have done so in the person of Jesus Christ. . . . The Creed's sequence of topics, and some of its phrases, express not only apostolic teaching, but also the explicit negation of Gnostic dualism at every point.[149]

So the Creed was great for dealing with the Gnostic heresy, but not with other doctrinal aberrations.

> Because of the early origin of its original form, it does not address some Christological issues defined in the Nicene and other Christian Creeds. It thus says nothing explicitly about the divinity of either Jesus or the Holy Spirit. This makes it acceptable to many Arians and Unitarians. Nor does it address many other theological questions which became objects of dispute centuries later.[150]

I have cited the foregoing simply to establish the fact that *The Apostles' Creed* is very good for its intended purposes as far as it goes, but it is certainly not comprehensive. I would like to point out one major omission which borders on distortion. The Creed begins, "I believe in God the Father Almighty, maker of heaven and earth / And in Jesus Christ,

---

149 Packer, *Affirming the Apostles' Creed,* 18–19.

150 Wikipedia, "Apostles' Creed," https://en.wikipedia.org/wiki/Apostles%27_Creed (accessed Sept. 9, 2018).

his only Son, our Lord…"[151] Notice it skips from *Creation* to *Christ*—from Genesis one to Matthew one. Even the casual observer will notice that there is quite a bit of Bible between those two chapters! Might that portion of the Tanakh have something of importance that should be fixed in our thinking—perhaps in a creed—that is vital to our getting the Big Story right? Luke Timothy Johnson gives content to this startling omission:

> Now we can consider more closely the content of the proposition, "God exists" as stated in the opening words of the creed. The structure of the creed reflects the Christian struggle to place a new experience of God through Jesus and the Holy Spirit in the church within a longer story, which is **nowhere stated** but **everywhere presupposed**. The creed grew out of the ancient confession of Israel, "Hear O Israel, the Lord your God is One" (Deut. 6:4). . . .
>
> It is of the first importance, then, to be clear that the story of God's work in and through Israel is the **implicit** premise for God's new work in Christ. The creed acknowledges this with its brief but meaningful **allusion** to the entire scriptural world in its confession of "one God," meaning the God of Israel. The creed begins with a **literary cross-reference—it says, in effect**, "to know what this means, go read the Old Testament." It is impossible to understand what the creed goes on to say about Jesus and the Holy Spirit apart from the Old Testament. (And, as we shall see, for Christians, it is also impossible fully to understand the Old Testament apart from Jesus.)[152] [emphases mine]

While I appreciate Johnson's scholarly defense and elucidation of the creed, it would seem that its opaque "*nowhere stated, everywhere presupposed, implicit, allusion, literary cross-reference, it says, in effect*" reference to something so vital as the content of the Tanakh and therefore Israel's role in

---

151 From The Traditional Version posted on the United Methodist Church website: http://www.umc.org/what-we-believe/apostles-creed-traditional-ecumenical?gclid=EAIaIQobChMIje-62o6f3QIVU0wNCh1viAp7EAAYASAAEgJDcPD_BwE. (accessed Sept. 10, 2018).

152 Johnson, *The Creed*, 72–73.

salvation history constitutes a grave weakness which would inevitably become lost on the average confessor.

The Missing "C"

A staple of Christian theology over the years has been to summarize the Big Story or canonical narrative of the Bible by using four words: *creation, fall, redemption*, and *restoration.* Relatively recently someone developed the helpful alliterative mnemonic: *creation, curse, cross,* and *consummation.* Like the omission in *The Apostles' Creed,* this grand narrative jumps again from Genesis (although this time from chapter three instead of one, which is an improvement) to Matthew.[153] I would like to suggest a *fifth* word beginning with the letter *C*, which would address this omission in standard Christian thinking about the Big Story and which needs to be explicitly confessed. That word is *covenant.*

Here I want to begin teasing out, in broad strokes, these five *C's* of the Big Story to see if we can get it, at least, a little less wrong if not completely "right."

Creation

In Genesis chapters one and two, we have the record of God creating everything that exists—that's ***C**reation.* While entire books have been

[153] An article which first appeared in *Leadership* magazine and was later posted on the *Christianity Today* website gave a brief description of each of these parts of the Big Story. For *Redemption* it had: "Thankfully the loving Creator who rightly shows Himself to be wrathful toward our sin is determined to turn evil and suffering we have caused into good that will be to His ultimate glory. So the next movement shows God implementing a master plan for redeeming His world and rescuing fallen sinners. In the Person of Jesus Christ, God Himself comes to renew the world and restore His people. The grand narrative of Scripture climaxes with the death and resurrection of Jesus." To be charitable, one might assume that when the author says that "the next movement [after the fall] shows God implementing a master plan for redeeming the world" he means to imply the content of the Tanakh vis-à-vis Israel and "climax[ing] with the death and resurrection of Jesus," but that is a mighty big assumption! Ed Stetzer, "The Big Story of Scripture (Creation, Fall, Redemption, and Restoration) in Pictures," *Leadership magazine*, Nov. 28, 2012, https://www.christianitytoday.com/edstetzer/2012/november/big-story-of-scripture-creation-fall-redemption.html (accessed Oct. 15, 2018).

written on this topic, I will limit myself to these two observations which are immediately relevant to The Big Story line and which are certainly not unique to me.

First, in making the first man, God takes material from the Earth, fashions it, then breathes into the inanimate body, and Adam becomes a living being. We are later told that God brings Eve out of Adam's side and the two are said to be made in God's image and likeness. Notice they are made of the Earth and for the Earth—a reinforcement of the New Earth idea touched on in chapter five.

Second, God gives authority to the humans he created to rule his creation and develop it to his glory. God is the unique *Creator,* but because we are made in his image—we can be *creative.* The story begins in a *garden* (Gen. 2:8), but ends in a *city* (Rev. 21:2).[154] Our first parents are not to just lay around in Paradise and eat mangoes; they are to tend the garden—shape and develop it (Gen. 2:15). And they are to do that with every aspect of the creation in every place of creation: "Be fruitful and multiply and fill the earth and subdue it" Gen. 1:28). This passage and the command expressed in it is sometimes referred to as the *Cultural* or *Dominion Mandate.* All of this speaks to the idea of the development of culture and the concept of progress—a unique gift of the Tanakh to humanity.[155] I am drawing attention to this aspect of creation because it tends to get lost in popular discussions of *Redemption/Cross* which tend to focus more narrowly on restoring the individual.

---

[154] This way of putting things (which is not original with me) is not meant to deny the existence of other entities (e.g., cities, nations, countrysides, etc.) in the New Earth besides the New Jerusalem. I believe that was made abundantly clear in chapter five. Rather, it is a short-hand way of expressing the idea that humanity's goal under God is not to, as in the words of a 1960's counterculture song, "get ourselves back to the garden,"* but to move forward toward a more developed creation. *Crosby, Stills, Nash & Young. Lyrics to "Woodstock," by Joni Mitchel. Genius Media Group, 2019, https://genius.com/Crosby-stills-nash-and-young-woodstock-lyrics (accessed Jan. 5, 2019).

[155] "Judaism repudiated the cyclic view of history held by all other ancient peoples and affirmed that it was a meaningful process leading to the gradual regeneration of humanity. This was the origin of the Western belief in progress..." Henry Bamford Parkes, *The Divine Order: Western Culture in the Middle Ages and the Renaissance* (New York, NY: Alfred A. Knopf, 1969), 14; cited in Dennis Prager and Joseph Telushkin, *The Nine Questions People Ask About Judaism* (New York, NY: Simon & Schuster, 1975, 1981), 30.

CURSE

In Genesis three, we see the fall of Adam and Eve into sin and the subsequent curse that falls on creation—that's ***C**urse.* Notice that God doesn't destroy Adam and Eve and start over. Consistent with all that we have said in the previous chapter, God's goal is not to destroy, but restore. So God brings judgment, but also makes a promise of future deliverance as he says to the serpent, "I will put enmity between you and the woman, and between your offspring [Lit. seed] and her offspring [Lit. seed]; he shall bruise your head, and you shall bruise his heel" (Gen. 3:15). This passage has long been cited by Christians as the protoevangelium (first gospel)[156] and already begins to bleed into the category of *Redemption.*

But before we move on, I want us to observe the link between the humans and the earth. The humans are not in proper relationship to God and that affects the earth. We see this theme developed under the *C* of *Covenant* where the fate of the people of Israel and the land are closely connected and later extended to the whole earth.[157]

What I have said here about *Creation* and *Curse* does not differ from the traditional accounts of the canonical narrative. But the introduction of the *Covenant* / "Israel and the Nations" theme into the traditional rendition of the Big Story and how that deepens our understanding of the *Cross* and the *Consummation* elements merits separate chapters for each.

---

156 For helpful elaborations see https://www.ligonier.org/learn/devotionals/proto-evangelium/and https://www.gotquestions.org/ protoevangelium.html (accessed Oct. 17, 2018).

157 We have a graphic picture of the people-land connection in Lev. 18:28, "lest the land vomit you out when you make it unclean, as it vomited out the nation that was before you." We also see a recurrent theme of the land being desolate when the people are disobedient as for instance in Lev. 26:31–33; "And I will lay your cities waste and will make your sanctuaries desolate, and I will not smell your pleasing aromas. And I myself will devastate the land, so that your enemies who settle in it shall be appalled at it. And I will scatter you among the nations, and I will unsheathe the sword after you, and your land shall be a desolation, and your cities shall be a waste." What was true of Israel as the prototypical nation is true of the whole world in relation to the earth: "For the creation was subjected to futility, not willingly, but because of him who subjected it, in hope that the creation itself will be set free from its bondage to corruption and obtain the freedom of the glory of the children of God" (Rom. 8:20–21).

SEVEN

THE REST OF THE STORY: *COVENANT*

Radio announcer Paul Harvey was known for initiating a story about some well-known person or incident, then revealing little known facts about the subject, and concluding with his signature sign off: "And now you know—the *rest* of the story." I'm afraid that the story of God's redemption of his creation is a bit like that. A majority of the world's population is tragically ignorant of it, many know its broad outlines, while a smaller number know more of the details. But as this book has tried to demonstrate, it seems that historically a key part of the story has been largely unknown—either through misinterpretation or neglect.

In the last chapter, we proposed that the Big Story of the Bible could best be represented by inserting into the traditional four *C's* a fifth one, *Covenant,* so that we now have: ***C****reation,* ***C****urse,* ***C****ovenant,* ***C****ross,* and ***C****onsummation.* We concluded it by briefly sketching out the implications of the first two *C's*. So now in these last three chapters I will sketch out the last three *C's*. And drawing on the best that current scholarship has to offer, I want to try to help you know, at least in part, "the rest of the story."

SCRIPTURAL CONTEXT

To place the *C* of ***C****ovenant* in its scriptural context, we need to briefly review the Genesis narrative from the fall of Adam and Eve into sin up to the call of Abram. So following the description of the fall in chapter three, humanity continues to spiral downward as we see Cain killing his brother, Lamech killing a man and boasting about it, and by Genesis six we read, "The Lord saw that the wickedness of man was great in the earth, and that every intention of the thoughts of his heart was only evil continually." God judges the earth and its inhabitants with a flood, but spares Noah and his family and representative animals. God reiterates the blessing spoken over Adam and Eve to Noah and his three sons: "Be fruitful and multiply and fill the earth" (Gen. 9:1). He then makes a covenant with humanity promising that he will never again judge the whole earth with a flood (Gen. 9:8–17). This *Noachide Covenant* as it has come to be called is the first mention of the word *covenant* in the Bible. Much could be said here but for our purposes it will suffice to note that again we see the theme of judgment with a view toward restoration at work. Genesis 10 and 11 tell the story of how the Nations, the ethnic peoples of the earth, came about. Rather than filling the earth as commanded by God, the peoples of the post-diluvian world confederated together to resist God's express command:

> "Come, let us build ourselves a city and a tower with its top in the heavens, and let us make a name for ourselves, lest we be dispersed over the face of the whole earth. And the Lord came down to see the city and the tower, which the children of man had built. And the Lord said, "Behold, they are one people, and they have all one language, and this is only the beginning of what they will do. And nothing that they propose to do will now be impossible for them. Come, let us go down and there confuse their language, so that they may not understand one another's speech." So the Lord dispersed them from there over the face of all the earth, and they left off building the city" (Gen. 11:4–8).

The implication of this passage seems to be that in their united rebellion, humanity would sink to even greater levels of evil than even before the flood[158] and so God has to scatter them to, as it were, break the synergy of collective, "creative" evil by dividing them. I would point out again that even this act of judgment has a redemptive side. He has thwarted the potentiality of their rebellious collaboration and, perhaps, has spared them the inevitable heartaches that come with unwieldy hierarchies—tyranny and slavery. Think of any empire in history—Lord Acton's "absolute power tends to corrupt absolutely" comes into play. Furthermore, He is giving them the high honor of being his image-bearers throughout the earth.

Nations Created

God scatters them by confounding their languages and in so doing new, separate Nations are *created.* It is vital to our understanding of God's purposes that this fact not be lost on us. God created *humanity* in Genesis one and two, but out of that common humanity he created the *Nations* in Genesis 10 and 11. The Bible specifically declares that God *made* or *created* the Nations:

> and that he will set you in praise and in fame and in honor high above **all nations that he has made**, and that you shall be a people holy to

---

158 Rabbi Jonathan Sacks, "A Drama in Four Acts," http://rabbisacks.org/drama-four-acts-noach-5779/. "The fourth is the enigmatic story of the Tower of Babel. The sin of its builders is unclear, but is indicated by two key words in the text. The story is framed, beginning and end, with the phrase kol ha'aretz, "the whole earth" (11:1, 8). In between, there is a series of similar sounding words: sham (there), shem (name), and shamayim (heaven). The story of Babel is a drama about the two key words of the first sentence of the Torah: "In the beginning, God created heaven (shamayim) and earth (aretz)" (1:1). Heaven is the domain of God; earth is the domain of man. By attempting to build a tower that would "reach heaven," the builders of Babel were humans trying to be like gods. This story seems to have little to do with responsibility, and to be focusing on a different issue than do the first three. However, not accidentally does the word responsibility suggest response-ability. The Hebrew equivalent, aĥrayut, comes from the word aĥer, meaning "an other." Responsibility is always a response to something or someone. In Judaism, it means response to the command of God. By attempting to reach heaven, the builders of Babel were in effect saying: we are going to take the place of God. We are not going to respond to His law or respect His boundaries, not going to accept His Otherness. We are going to create an environment where we rule, not Him, where the Other is replaced by Self. Babel is the failure of ontological responsibility – the idea that something beyond us makes a call on us."

> the LORD your God, as he promised. (Deut. 26:19)

> **All the nations you have made** shall come and worship before you, O Lord, and shall glorify your name. (Ps. 89:6)

> And **he made from one man every nation of mankind** to live on all the face of the earth, having determined allotted periods and the boundaries of their dwelling place. (Acts 17:26)

The above are just a few of many such passages which attest to the fact that God created the Nations—and these creations of his will not be eliminated or transmogrified beyond all recognition—but rather eventually redeemed, renewed, and restored, as will the rest of his creation.

ISRAEL CREATED

It is within the context of God creating the nations that we then read in Genesis 12 that he specifically creates a special nation for special purposes—the Jewish people or Israel:

> Now the LORD said to Abram, "Go from your country and your kindred and your father's house to the land that I will show you. And **I will make of you** a great nation..." (Gen. 12:1-2)

> But now thus says the LORD, **he who created you**, O Jacob, he who formed you, O Israel: "Fear not, for I have redeemed you; I have called you by name, you are mine. (Isaiah 43:1)

The above are just a few of many such passages which attest to the fact that God created Israel—and like all of the other Nations and all of his other good creations, it will not be eliminated or transmogrified beyond all recognition—but eventually redeemed, renewed, and restored.

With Genesis 12 we find a major shift in the biblical narrative. Genesis 1–11 is about God's dealings with humanity—first as a unified, if we could say, homogenized whole, then later in the form of "the Nations." As though to set the stage for the decisive transition that occurs in chapter 12, the structure of Genesis 1–11 clearly highlights four moments in human history when catastrophic sin occurs with concomitant judgment. Jonathan Sacks calls this "A Drama in Four Acts": Adam and Eve, Cain and Abel, Noah and his ark, and the Tower of Babel.[159]

Beginning with Genesis 12 we see something new. It is not a complete ignoring or turning away from general humanity in the Nations, but the calling of a single individual through whom God will create another nation, yet one that is distinctively different from all the rest—in order to "be a blessing" to the rest.[160] That this nation is distinctively different from the other Nations is highlighted repeatedly in the Tanakh. Below are just a few representative examples:

> Behold, a people dwelling alone, and not counting itself among the nations! (Num. 23:9b)

> He declares his word to Jacob, his statutes and rules to Israel. He has not dealt thus with any other nation; they do not know his rules. (Ps. 147:19–20)

> You only have I known of all the families of the earth; therefore I will punish you for all your iniquities. (Amos 3:2)

ISRAEL'S CHOSENNESS

That Israel is chosen and set apart to be a special servant of the Lord that He will use to touch the Nations is made equally clear.

> I will bless those who bless you [Abram], and him who dishonors you I will curse, and in you all the families of the earth shall be blessed." (Gen. 12:3)

---

159 Ibid.

160 "Genesis 12:2–3 pointedly declared that Abraham's name, his blessing, and his being made into a great nation was for the purpose of being a blessing to all the peoples of the earth." Walter A. Kaiser, "The Great Commission in the Old Testament," in the *International Journal of Frontier Missions*, vol. 13:1 Jan.–Mar. 1996.

> May God be gracious to us and bless us and make his face to shine upon us, Selah, that your way may be known on earth, your saving power among all nations. Let the peoples praise you, O God; let all the peoples praise you! (Ps. 67:1–3)

This choosing of Israel by God has been referred to by some in the history of theology as "the scandal of particularity" and begs for an explanation. This is all the more relevant in our age which elevates that which is egalitarian above virtually all other considerations. Mercifully, God's revelation in the Scriptures gives us at least some understanding of the mystery of his sovereign will in this matter.

I decided not to try to answer so important a question as "Why Did God Choose Israel?" in my own words. I have at my disposal many good treatises on the subject, but since my aim in this book is both brevity and clarity, I chose the following excerpt from an article addressing it by the editorial staff of One For Israel. As an organization comprised of Jewish people who believe that Jesus is the promised Jewish Messiah, I believe they offer a thoughtful, thorough, and sensitive answer to a difficult question that combines some of the best responses of the synagogue as well as the church.

> We often think of God's choice of Israel as an honour and privilege, but it also carries a heavy responsibility. More than one Jewish person has verbally wished that the choice had landed on another people group instead. God warns Israel, *"You only have I chosen of all the families of the earth; therefore I will punish you for all your sins" (Amos 3:1–2).*
>
> God calls Israel to a higher standard, precisely because of his unique revelation and choice of them. Just as a judge might "make an example" out of a criminal, Israel serves as an example and a lesson to the world. The curses and punishments in Deuteronomy promised to Israel if they fail are eye-watering in their severity and extremity.
>
> Psalm 147 declares: *"He has revealed his word to Jacob, his laws and decrees to Israel. He has done this for no other nation."* God wanted us all to have access to the scriptures – the "oracles of God" as Paul calls them – the precious words of God to the world. He also wanted to bring his Messiah into the world through a people group. Through humanity it-

> self. A personal delivery. The Jewish people are trustees, guardians and messengers of these gifts to the world.
>
> Israel may be the nation that was chosen, but they have been chosen for a reason. The reason is not merited by themselves, but God's reason is to bless all the nations on the earth.
>
> God wanted a 'flagship' nation that was an example to the world – not of how they behave, but of how he behaves.
>
> We can learn by observing the twists and turns of the love story between God and Israel what kind of character it is that we are following. We can see his faithfulness. We can see his standards. We can see his compassionate love and mercy, as well as his jealousy and wrath when he is rejected for other lovers.
>
> The Bible cannot be understood without appreciating the place of Israel in his grand scheme – from beginning to end. Indeed, looking through the lens of his dealings with Israel is like a key that unlocks the scriptures.
>
> However, a cursory glance backwards through history shows how time and time again, while the people of Israel may be the object of God's undying affection, they are also targeted for special hatred – the unquenchable, Satanic drive to annihilate them continues throughout the generations. It is enough to make anyone envious of the chosen people retreat from that position with gratitude.[161]

I, for one, have undying gratitude for the Jewish people for who they are, what they have endured, and what they have given to the world. Most of all, I am thankful for how they have indeed served as "a 'flagship' nation that was an example to the world – not of how they behave, but of how he behaves." Through his dealings with Israel, in both verbal expressions of love, powerful deliverances, and abundant blessings, as well as rebukes and judgments, God has begun to "get through" to the Nations (of which I am a part) in ways that He apparently was not before He chose Israel, as the first eleven chapters of

---

[161] Editorial Staff of One For Israel, "Why Did God Choose Israel?" https://www.oneforisrael.org/bible-based-teaching-from-israel/why-did-god-choose-israel/ (accessed Nov. 24, 2018).

Genesis make clear.[162]

LIGHT TO THE NATIONS

The Tanakh gives repeated testimony to the fact that Israel served as "a light for the nations" (Isaiah 49:6) to show them the greatness of the one true God. We only need to recall the stories of all of the patriarchs and matriarchs in their contacts with the Pharaoh's and Abimelek's, or Joseph with Pharaoh, or Moses with the Egyptians, or Joshua with the Canaanites as well as the succeeding Judges, or David with the Nations round about Israel. All of these demonstrated the truth God declared through Moses to Israel just before they entered the promised land:

> See, I have taught you statutes and rules, as the LORD my God commanded me, that you should do them in the land that you are entering to take possession of it. Keep them and do them, for that will be your wisdom and your understanding in the sight of the peoples, who, when they hear all these statutes, will say, 'Surely this great nation is a wise and understanding people.' For what great nation is there that has a god so near to it as the LORD our God is to us, whenever we call upon him? And what great nation is there, that has statutes and rules so righteous as all this law that I set before you today? (Deut. 4:5–8)

We may take from this passage that God blessed Israel primarily in two ways: (1) by making himself uniquely accessible to them through all that pertained to the tabernacle and later the temple, and (2) by giving them the Torah which provided guidance and wisdom concerning every aspect of human endeavor in such a way that life and blessing would be maximized. This dynamic came into fullest expression at the time of

---

162 A good father loves each of his children in special, unique ways precisely because each one is different. God's particular love for Israel demonstrates that he has particular loves for each nation and individual. The God of the Bible does not love with a generic benevolent tolerance. He shouts with joy over Israel as a nation and over David's, Joseph's and Sarah's as individuals. He also shouts for joy over a redeemed Mexico and over individual Juan's, Carlos's, and Carlita's. The same is true with Germans, Pakistanis, and all the ethnos. But the nations can't imagine getting their own unique love from the Father, so they try to destroy or displace Israel.

King Solomon's reign whose glory became legendary in his own lifetime. It would seem that the Queen of Sheba's response, as a representative of the Nations, to what God had done in Israel through Solomon, demonstrates the validity of God's plan to superabundantly bless Israel and through Israel to provoke the Nations to, could we say, envy:

> And she said to the king, "The report was true that I heard in my own land of your words and of your wisdom, but I did not believe the reports until I came and my own eyes had seen it. And behold, the half was not told me. Your wisdom and prosperity surpass the report that I heard. Happy are your men! Happy are your servants, who continually stand before you and hear your wisdom! Blessed be the Lord your God, who has delighted in you and set you on the throne of Israel! Because the Lord loved Israel forever, he has made you king, that you may execute justice and righteousness." (1 Kings 10:6–9)

How marvelous! God's special nation Israel is blessed and through her God is making himself known to the Nations. If we can allow ourselves a moment of indulgence in "sanctified imagination," the words from the mouth of Sheba's queen must have been music to God's ears! If only it could have lasted!

THE NEED FOR A MESSIAH

For all of the glory in the history of the Jewish people, there is also the discordant note of disobedience to the covenant. This is certainly not because they are any more wicked than anyone else on the face of the earth, but rather because they share with all humanity the condition described by Jeremiah, "The heart is deceitful above all things, and desperately sick; who can understand it?" (Jer. 17:9). Even when Solomon becomes king, Israel has wealth beyond imagination, is at peace with her neighbors, and the Nations come to see the glory of his kingdom, it cannot last because of the weakness of Solomon.

The Bible is a remarkable work on many counts, but a major one is that it doesn't whitewash the sins of its heroes. And that central, consistent problem begs to be addressed. It is certainly addressed through the sacrificial system that is so integral to the life of Israel, but it is also addressed by two other covenantal initiatives from God:

1) **Davidic Covenant:** There is the announcement of what has come to be called the *Davidic Covenant* (2 Samuel 7) in which God promises to establish the house of David forever by perpetually having one of his offspring ruling as king over all of Israel. From the subsequent development of this *Davidic Covenant* by the prophets emerges the picture of a Messianic king who will not only deliver and rule over his people Israel, but "he shall speak peace to the nations" and rule over them—"his rule shall be from sea to sea, and from the River to the ends of the earth" (Zech. 9:23). Indeed, at least one strand of Talmudic thought states, *"All the prophets prophesied not but of the days of the Messiah"* (Sanhedrin 99a).
2) **New Covenant:** There is the announcement of a *New Covenant* which contrasts it with the one made with Israel at Sinai. Nothing negative is said about the content of that Mosaic Covenant; after all, it is from God. But it does highlight the problem of the people—their continual unwillingness/inability to keep the covenant. Thus, the need for a *new* covenant that would somehow deal with the sinful hearts of the people:

> "Behold, the days are coming, declares the LORD, when I will make a new covenant with the house of Israel and the house of Judah, not like the covenant that I made with their fathers on the day when I took them by the hand to bring them out of the land of Egypt, my covenant that they broke, though I was their husband, declares the LORD. For this is the covenant that I will make with the house of Israel after those days, declares the LORD: I will put my law within them, and I will write it on their hearts. And I will be their God, and they shall be my people. And no longer shall each one teach his neighbor and each his brother, saying, 'Know the LORD,' for

> they shall all know me, from the least of them to the greatest, declares the LORD. For I will forgive their iniquity, and I will remember their sin no more." (Jer. 31:31–34)

The ideas and ideals surrounding both the *Davidic Covenant* and the *New Covenant* perhaps find united expression in the vision of the prophets as *The Messenger of the Covenant:* "Behold, I send my messenger, and he will prepare the way before me. And the Lord whom you seek will suddenly come to his temple; and *the messenger of the covenant* in whom you delight, behold, he is coming, says the LORD of hosts" (Mal. 3:1).[163] The NT identifies this Messianic figure as Jesus of Nazareth. To the impact of his appearing on "Israel and the Nations" under the heading of *Cross* we now turn.

163 Andrew S. Malone, "Is The Messiah Announced In Malachi 3:1?" *Tyndale Bulletin* 57.2 (2006) 215–228, https://legacy.tyndalehouse.com/tynbul/Library/TynBull_2006_57_2_04_ Malone_MessiahinMal3.pdf (accessed Sept. 9, 2018).

EIGHT

The Rest of the Story: *Cross*

A Wrong Turn in the Big Story

We observed previously that in summarizing the Big Story of Scripture, theologians have historically placed the person and work of Jesus of Nazareth under the heading of *Redemption*—or to keep the alliteration going—***C**ross*. And it is here where a major wrong turn in the Big Story occurs. From Genesis 12 to Malachi 4,[164] we have the continual theme first announced in the Abrahamic Covenant of—"Israel and the Nations." The two competing Big Story canonical narratives which we examined previously—Supersessionism/Replacement Theology and Dispensationalism—view the coming of Christ as a radical break from this schema. Replacement Theology sees Israel as a temporary expedient whose sole purpose for existence is to deliver the Messiah to the world. Once that task had been accomplished, Israel qua Israel was no longer needed. As Stuart Dauermann laments, "Israel should not be viewed as the Parcel Post People of God that delivers the package of salvation to the Church and then recedes from the scene….ethnic Israel is most often reduced to the status of a vestigial organ that was once useful but now unnecessary."[165] Dispensationalism posits that Jesus offered the

---

164 Here I am using the order of the books historically used by the church. The Tanakh ends with what is referred to by English speakers as 2 Chronicles.

165 Carl Kinbar, "Messianic Jews and Scripture," in *Introduction to Messianic Judaism*, 64. Someone also used the image of the booster rockets which fall away once a shuttle is launched.

kingdom to Israel, but Israel in its representative leaders rejected the offer. So God postponed his *earthly* kingdom program with Israel (one Bible teacher compared this action with pushing the pause button on a video player) and started doing a brand new thing by creating a *heavenly* entity called the *church* consisting primarily of Gentiles. While these two systems differ radically from one another, they share in common the idea that with the coming of the Jewish Messiah, God is not doing anything with the Jewish people as a people now. N. T. Wright explains why these approaches are scripturally untenable:

> If God called and commissioned Israel to be the light to the nations, how will that plan now go forward? If God established his covenant through Abraham as the means by which the world would be made right, but if the covenant people have let him down, is God now going to abandon the covenant, forget Israel, and do things by a different route? At this point the usual reading of Romans—reflecting the traditional view of the church—has answered: yes! God has parked his broken-down car in a side road somewhere and has completed the journey on foot. He has jettisoned the covenant with Israel and has instead intervened in person, in Jesus. This is how the "gospel" is presented by many Christians today, including those who use the "Romans road." As we have seen, that explanation simply goes like this: we sinned, God sent Jesus to die for us, we are saved. No mention of Israel. But when you leave out Israel, your shortened story will easily tip over into a non-Jewish way of thinking, into, as we have seen, a platonic view of the ultimate goal ("heaven")….And at some point this non-Jewish story all too often turns into an anti-Jewish story. That was a risk in Paul's day too. This is why he wrote Romans 9-11.[166]

---

166 N. T. Wright, *The Day The Revolution Began: Reconsidering the Meaning of Jesus's Crucifixion* (New York, NY: Harper-Collins Publishers, 2016), 311–312. While I am very appreciative of much of this world class scholar's work, in fairness to him and the reader, I must also point out that he does not share the understanding of the NT's usage of the term *Israel* that is set forth in this book. For example, he writes on page 236: "…those who belong to Jesus are now part of the 'new creation,' 'God's Israel.' (That latter phrase is controversial, since many readers have resisted the implication that Paul would use the word 'Israel' to refer to the whole people of Israel's Messiah, whether they were Jewish or non-Jewish. But the interpretation I have given seems clearly in line with the thought of the letter as a whole.)"

JESUS FOR ISRAEL AND THE NATIONS

To avoid the inadequacies of both Supersessionism and Dispensationalism, it is especially at this point in our thinking, when interpreting the meaning of the coming of Jesus in fulfillment of God's promises, that we need to remind ourselves of the hermeneutical principle of "Begin With the End in Mind" set forth in chapter five. For if it is true that we see "Israel and the Nations" at the end of the Bible and "Israel and the Nations" all the way through the roughly first three quarters of the Bible, then it would behoove us to at least consider the possibility that this same theme continues in the portion of the Bible we have been referring to as the NT. Consider these representative examples:

- **TWO Genealogies:** In its opening pages, we find in Matthew chapter one a genealogy in which Jesus is identified with Abraham and David, i.e., highlighting his Jewish identity and mission to his people. But in Luke chapter three we find his genealogy presented to us in such a way that he is also identified with Adam, i.e., with all of humanity or the Nations.
- **A DUAL Mission:** Within these same early chapters, we read of aged Simeon who speaks at the dedication of Jesus in the temple at Jerusalem: "Lord, now you are letting your servant depart in peace, according to your word; for my eyes have seen your salvation that you have prepared in the presence of all peoples, **a light for revelation to the Gentiles, and for glory to your people Israel**" (Luke 2:29–32). Here again we see the joined-at-the-hip dual mission to "Israel and the Nations" clearly and unambiguously stated.
- **Parabolic Life of Israel AND Adam:** Since at least the time of Irenaeus in the second century, the idea of Jesus's life recapitulating that of Adam has been recognized as an important aspect of his identification with all of humanity in order to redeem it.[167] But if one looks more closely, the theme of Jesus recapitulating the history of his people Israel is even more telling, e.g., fleeing the Promised Land to Egypt, coming out of Egypt, going through the

[167] See chapter three under **Irenaeus** for an elaboration of his idea of recapitulation.

waters of Jordan, sojourning in the wilderness, going up on a mountain to give clarification to the law of God, etc.[168]

- **Ultimate Israelite AND Adam:** Although not specifically stated in the NT, in theological circles Jesus is often referred to as the *ultimate* or *ideal* Israelite. In his solitary person he walks in obedience to God's commands in a way that no one else in Israel's long history ever did. I believe this is a fair inference from the Scriptures. But then the unjustified move is made of asserting that therefore, God has no more use for Israel as a people. As one writer puts it, "Only one Jew is essential to the Church and that is the Jew Jesus."[169] This is the Parcel Post People of God view referenced above. But, whereas the construct of Jesus as the ultimate Israelite is drawn from inference, the Bible explicitly calls him "the last (or ultimate) Adam" (2 Cor. 15:45), yet no one draws from this fact the conclusion that therefore God has no more need of the children of Adam, humanity—the Nations. In sum, the person and work of Jesus as representative of Israel and all of humanity or the Nations does not do away with either.[170]

- **King of Israel AND the Nations:** Jesus is referred to as "King of the Jews" (e.g., Matt. 27:37). But He is also referred to as "King of Kings" and "Lord of Lords" (Rev. 19:16)—a reference to the Nations.

- **Light THROUGH Renewed Israel to ENLIGHTEN the Nations:** In the Tanakh, Israel is called to be "a light for the nations, that my salvation may reach to the end of the earth" (Isa. 49:6). The NT depicts Jesus as the Jewish Messiah who is called to be "a

---

168 I must emphasize here that what is written above is merely representative, and by no means exhaustive, of the parallels between the history of Israel and the life of Jesus. For a more complete account see Dan Juster, *Jewish Roots: Understanding Your Jewish Faith* (Shippensburg, PA: Destiny Image Publishers, Inc., 2013), 70–72.

169 Paul M. van Buren, *Discerning the Way* (New York, NY: Seabury, 1980), 155; cited in *Introduction to Messianic Judaism*, 15.

170 "That Paul discusses Jesus and Israel in Romans 9–11 shows the importance of both. It also shows that Israel's identity and role are not absorbed into the person of Christ in a way that makes national Israel irrelevant. Jesus is the ultimate Israelite, and Israel is significant as a people and nation. The relationship of Jesus to Israel is not that of an antitype who makes an inferior type irrelevant. Instead, it is that of corporate headship—the representative head of Israel (Jesus) restores the many (national Israel)....Because of Jesus, the true Israelite, promises made to Israel will be fulfilled over the course of his two comings." Vlach, "A Non-Typological Future-Mass-Conversion View," 67.

light for revelation to the Gentiles" (Lk. 2:32). Then the Jewish Paul states that he has the same mandate: "For so the Lord has commanded us, saying, 'I have made you a light for the Gentiles, that you may bring salvation to the ends of the earth'" (Acts 13:48, cf. Isa. 49:6). A supersessionist reading of this verse would suggest a radical disjunction from what has gone before. In this understanding, Paul is a representative of something called *the Church* which has nothing to do with *Israel* and which has now taken over Israel's vocation to be a light to the Nations. But in a post-supersessionist[171] reading we see a continuation of God's theme of "Israel and the Nations." That is, the nation Israel is called to be a light to the Nations, but often fails because of sin. Her Messiah comes to bring her the freedom from sin and empowerment through the spirit of holiness needed in order to be all that she was meant to be as a witness to the Nations. Then we see a Jewish Paul along with other renewed sons and daughters of Israel successfully and much more extensively than at any previous time in Israel's history carrying out her mandate to be "a light for the nations." And in the marvelous plan of God, those of the Nations who respond to the light of the Messiah will themselves enter into this prophetic task of being "a light for the nations" as they are now described as "children of God without blemish in the midst of a crooked and twisted generation, among whom you shine as lights in the world" (Phil. 2:15).

- **Patriarchal Promises CONFIRMED to Israel AND Gentiles Receive Mercy:** Paul writes: "For I tell you that Christ became a servant to the circumcised to show God's truthfulness, in order to confirm the promises given to the patriarchs, **and** in order that the Gentiles might glorify God for his mercy" (Rom. 15:8–9a). Again we see Christ having a dual mission: he came to confirm

[171] "Supersessionism names a theological view whether explicitly or implicitly which believes the church has replaced ethnic Israel covenantally. Whereas evangelical post-supersessionism asserts that an evangelical view of Scripture demands we hold a view of God's continuing covenantal love and commitment to ethnic Israel in the age of the church and beyond. There are post-supersessionistic perspectives with which an evangelical theology cannot abide, such as one that espouses a two-covenant theology. But an evangelical post-supersessionism would reject this position as inconsistent with the NT witness of the necessity of the Messiah for Jew and Gentile alike." Joel Willitts, "Evangelical Post-Supersessionism," on Patheos blog, Dec. 9, 2013, http://www.patheos.com/blont/ euangelion/2013/12/evangelical-post-supersessionism/ (accessed Oct. 21, 2018).

the patriarchal promises to the Jewish people AND to bless the Nations.[172] Notice further that the text says Christ came "to *confirm* the promises given to the patriarchs." It doesn't say he came to *reinterpret, spiritualize,* or *transfer* the promises.[173]

JESUS'S CONGREGATION

The theme of "Israel and the Nations" continuing to run through the NT invites the discussion of how we should think about the entity's called *the church* and *Israel.* Moses spoke of a time when,

> "The LORD your God will raise up for you a prophet like me from among you, from your brothers—it is to him you shall listen—just as you desired of the LORD your God at Horeb on the day of the assembly, when you said, 'Let me not hear again the voice of the LORD my God or see this great fire any more, lest I die.' And the LORD said to me, 'They are right in what they have spoken. I will raise up for them a

---

[172] In verses 9b through 12 he cites passages from the Law, Psalms, and Prophets which all predict the Gentiles coming to worship Israel's God.

[173] Ps. 105:8-11 says: "He remembers his covenant forever, the word that he commanded, for a thousand generations, the covenant that he made with Abraham, his sworn promise to Isaac, which he confirmed to Jacob as a statute, to Israel as an everlasting covenant, saying, 'To you I will give the land of Canaan as your portion for an inheritance.'" Gerhard von Rad points out that "Of all the promises made to the patriarchs it was that of the land that was the most prominent and decisive."* It is exegetically untenable to quote verses like Joshua 21:45, "Not one word of all the good promises that the LORD had made to the house of Israel had failed; all came to pass," to try to make the case that the land promises have been fulfilled when even at that time Israel did not possess all of its inheritance. The same is true of 1 Kings 8:56, "Blessed be the LORD who has given rest to his people Israel, according to all that he promised. Not one word has failed of all his good promise, which he spoke by Moses his servant." Furthermore, to whatever extents at various times Israel occupied portions of the land promised to them, it was only for relatively brief periods of time. Further, it will not do to say that the promise of the land has been spiritualized by quoting a verse such as Hebrews 12:22 "But you have come to Mount Zion and to the city of the living God, the heavenly Jerusalem, and to innumerable angels in festal gathering..." and say that all the earthly land promises in the Tanakh have now been spiritualized as "heavenly." The concept of a heavenly Jerusalem corresponding to the earthly Jerusalem has been present in Jewish thought for a long time and the existence of the heavenly does not do away with or dismiss the earthly. For example, see Harav Baruch Gigi, *The Heavenly Jerusalem and the Earthly Jerusalem*, https://www.etzion.org.il/en/heavenly-jerusalem-and-earthly-jerusalem (accessed Jan. 28, 2019). *Gerhard von Rad, *The Problem of the Hexateuch and Other Essays,* trans. E. W. Trueman Sicken (London: Oliver & Boyd, 1966), 79, cited in McDermott, *The New Christian Zionism,* 48.

> prophet like you from among their brothers. And I will put my words in his mouth, and he shall speak to them all that I command him. And whoever will not listen to my words that he shall speak in my name, I myself will require it of him.'" (Deut. 18:15–19)

These verses do not verify Jesus as God. Only as a prophet

The NT asserts both implicitly and explicitly that Jesus of Nazareth was this prophet like Moses that God had promised to send (cf. John 5:46; Acts 3:22–23; 7:37). Moses led a *congregation* in the wilderness. Jesus announced that he would also build and lead "*my congregation*" (Matt. 16:18)—made up of those who would listen to his words. The underlying Hebrew and Greek words respectively translated *congregation* are cognate, i.e., related.[174] It is right at this point that we must take special care in how we understand the implications of what is going on here. Clearly, a change has occurred. There was a listening to Moses; now there is to be a listening to Jesus.[175]

---

[174] The Qahal (Hebrew: קהל) was a theocratic organizational structure in ancient Israelite society according to the Hebrew Bible. The Hebrew word qahal, which is a close etymological relation of the name of Qoheleth (Ecclesiastes), comes from a root meaning "convoked [group]"; its Arabic cognate, قال qāla, means to speak. Where the Masoretic Text uses the term qahal, the Septuagint usually uses the Koine Greek term ekklesia, ἐκκλησία, which means "summoned group" (literally, "they who are called out"). However, in one particular part of the Priestly Code, the Septuagint instead uses the term συναγωγή [synagogue], literally meaning "gathering." Wikipedia, "Qahal," https://en.wikipedia.org/wiki/Qahal (accessed on Oct. 24, 2018).

[175] The Pharisees were correct in understanding that the Torah invited/needed "filling out." For example, God commanded "you shall not do any work" (Ex. 20:8) on the Sabbath. But the question naturally arises, "What constitutes work?" The scribes and Pharisees of the Second Temple period began giving answers to that question in the form of Halakhic rulings which they believed were in accordance with or were an unfolding of an Oral Torah given to Moses at the same time the Written Torah was given. They did not view their work as denying or conflicting with Moses, but rather amplifying and clarifying. Likewise, Jesus does not contradict Moses. Rather, as the prophet who is like unto Moses, i.e., the Messiah, he comes in his person, words, and deeds, to both "fill out" and *fulfill* all the implications of that which God through Moses delivered to his people. For an expression of this concept from a non-Messianic Jewish perspective see David Novak, "Supersessionism Hard and Soft," *First Things*, Feb. 2019, 27–31: There is a better way [to view the origins of Judaism and Christianity], and it relies on a different kind of soft supersessionism. To formulate this approach, we need to correct a historical mistake many Christians and Jews make about the origins of both Christianity and Judaism. The mistake rests in the assumption that Christianity (however "softly") comes after Judaism. For Christians, that usually means Christianity arises from an already existing Judaism, bringing it *up* to a higher, fuller level of human existence before God. For Jews, conversely, that usually means that Christianity comes after, bringing Judaism *down* to a lower, more diluted level of human existence before God.

The Supersessionist infers that God is permanently done with ethnic Israel who found their national shape and identity in Moses. The Dispensationalist infers that God is temporarily done with ethnic Israel, puts his program with them on hold, and now inaugurates a brand new program with the Gentiles (and a few Jewish individuals) which is totally unrelated to national Israel. In contrast to these two historic theological constructs, scholars who are working with the emerging new paradigm of "Israel and the Nations" see the change as one that is not *away from* national Israel—but *within* national Israel.

Israel's Changing Modes

Actually, this kind of change should not take us completely by surprise. One way of reading the Tanakh is to see a pattern of God working faithfully with this chosen people through a variety of *changing* modes of being. Consider these different "states" in which they have existed in relation to the Nations:

> **Patriarchs:** The patriarchs, matriarchs, and eventually the twelve sons sojourn in the land of promise with varying degrees of tension and peace with peoples of the Nations.

But Christianity did not *come out of* Judaism, whether for good (the Christian supersessionist view) or for ill (the Jewish supersessionist view). In truth, *both* Christianity and Rabbinic Judaism come out of, and thereby supersede, a religion based on the Hebrew Bible, plus some developments coming from the elaborative interpretations of Second Temple Jewish theology, the time after the final books of the Hebrew Bible were written but before the first century of Christianity. This religion could be called "Hebraic Monotheism." It is neither Judaism nor Christianity, at least as we know them from the second century on. Judaism and Christianity have been continually superseding this ancient religion. Both have done so without forgetting their ever-present, ever-necessary foundation in Hebraic Monotheism.

Thus, it is incorrect to say that Jews only have the "Old Testament," while Christians have both the Old Testament *and* the "New Testament." Christians and Jews accept the Old Testament/Hebrew Bible as interpreted by Second Temple Jewish theology to be their foundational revelation. This is what we have in common. In addition, both Christians and Jews have a "new testament." For Christians, this "new testament" is the book by that very name, plus the ongoing tradition of the Church (its *magisterium)* extending that new testament into the present. For Jews, our "new testament" is the "Oral Torah" *(torah she-b'al peh),* written down in the Talmud (and related canonical rabbinic texts) but constantly being extended as *tradition* up until the latest Jewish teachings. So, just as the Talmud could be called the "Jewish New Testament," so also the New Testament could be called the "Christian Talmud." In fact, in both the New Testament and the Talmud, there is nothing of any significance being taught that does not seek a basis in the Old Testament, or what Jews call the Written Torah *(torah she-bi-khtiv).*

Egypt: The children of Israel dwell in peace in the nation of Egypt under Joseph's care and then in slavery under Pharaoh.

Wilderness: The children of Israel receive the gift of the Torah which begins to entirely reshape their corporate life, are provided supernatural sustenance in the form of manna, journey with a mixed multitude from the nation of Egypt who cause problems, and fight Amalekites who attack them.

Judges: The children of Israel are now somewhat separated from each other according to their tribal allotments and when in disobedience, the Nations around them bring them into bondage. Then, periodically, Deliverers or Judges are raised up by God in response to his people's cries.

United Monarchy: First under Saul, then David, the tribes come into a coordinated confederation and the Nations immediately around them are subdued (and in some cases are even friendly, e.g., King Hiram of Tyre). And under Solomon Israel reaches the pinnacle of expressing God's plan to superabundantly bless Israel and through Israel to provoke the Nations to envy as described in the previous chapter.

Divided Monarchy: Because of the disobedience of Solomon, the "unthinkable" occurs. The chosen people of God experience a major *national* division into two distinct nations, the Southern Kingdom consisting of Judah and Benjamin and the Northern Kingdom consisting of the other ten tribes who choose not to follow the kingly line of David. At times they even fight each other!

Northern Kingdom Destroyed: A further "unthinkable" occurs when the Assyrians invade and carry away captive the people of the Northern Kingdom of Israel and it no longer exists as a nation.

Southern Kingdom Destroyed: Again, another "unthinkable" occurs when the Babylonians invade, destroy the holy temple and city, and carry away captive the people of the Southern Kingdom. Thus it also no longer exists as an independent, sovereign nation.

Babylonian Exile: The "unthinkable" continues as the people of the Southern Kingdom dwell outside of the promised land, in the land of one of the Nations—Babylon, for the first time since their ancestors left Egypt 900 years previously. Even more shocking, they are living without tabernacle or temple—the visible expressions of God being with them.

The Return: After 70 years, a mere remnant of the people of God consisting of at least a few representatives from all twelve tribes (and Levites), returns to the land to rebuild the temple and Jerusalem. Now, for the first time in their history, there is a major *geographical* division in the people of God as many more live outside the promised land among the Nations in what is called the Diaspora than inside of it.

The Second Temple Period: The people of God no longer stand as an independent nation among the Nations, but now live under four successive Empires: Babylonian, Persian, Grecian, and Roman.[176] A combination of political, spiritual, and cultural pressures, both internal and external, lead to major *cultural/spiritual* divisions of the people into various "parties" so that by the time of the first century of the common era we find groups such as the Pharisees, Sadducees, Essences, Zealots, and "the people of the land"[177] among others; a phenomenon for which Rabbi Jacob Neusner proposed justification for using the plural "Judaisms" rather than Judaism to describe accurately.[178]

---

[176] Of course, the domination by Babylon began and ended before the Return, but I include it because it was the first instance of empire domination which led to the subsequent ones. Also, it is included in Daniel's visions of four empires (Daniel 2 and 7) dominating Israel. There was a brief semi-respite from this domination as the Grecian Empire grew weak and Rome was just beginning to rise as a power. In the wake of the Maccabean revolt from Greek domination, there followed a nearly 100-year period of semi-autonomy for Israel under the Hasmonian dynasty. However, it was marked by constant internal conflict which eventually ended in one party inviting Rome to come in to settle the dispute. Rome gladly complied and took over!

[177] "In the Tanakh, the term 'the people of the land' (Hebrew *am ha'aretz*) refers to a special social group or caste within the kingdom of Judah. . . . Usage of the term *am ha'aretz* in the Hebrew Bible has little connection to usage in the Hasmonean period and hence in the Mishnah. The *am ha'aretz* were of two types, the *am ha'aretz le-mitzvot*, Jews disparaged for not scrupulously observing the commandments, and the *am ha'aretz la-Torah*, those stigmatized as ignoramuses for not having studied the Torah at all." Wikipedia, "Am ha'aretz," https://en.wikipedia.org/wiki/Am_ha%27aretz#Tanakh (accessed Nov. 1, 2018).

[178] "...he courted controversy by asserting that multiple Judaisms, arising from local conditions, coexisted in the period after the fall of the Second Temple in Jerusalem in A.D. 70. He put forth this thesis in *Judaism: The Evidence of the Mishnah* (1981), which the religious scholar Jonathan Z. Smith called "a Copernican revolution in rabbinical studies." N.Y. Times, obituary for Jacob Neusner, https://www.nytimes.com/2016/10/11/us/jacob-neusner-judaic-scholar-who-forged-interfaith-bonds-dies-at-84.html. For a rebuttal of this view see Seth Schwartz, "How Many Judaisms Were There?" *Journal of Ancient Judaism: Volume 2, Issue 2,* 2011, 208–238. https://doi.org/10.13109/jaju.2011.2.2.208 (both accessed Oct. 31, 2018).

Throughout all of these various *changes* in Israel's "mode of existence" and the resulting changes in her relationship to the Nations, one factor remained *constant*—the Lord's unfailing covenant love (Heb. *chesed*). He rebukes, chastises, and prunes, but does not *ultimately*[179] ever abandon his people: "For the LORD will not forsake his people, for his great name's sake, because it has pleased the LORD to make you a people for himself" (1 Sam. 12:22; cf. 1 Kin. 6:13; Ps. 94:14; Ezra 9:9; Neh. 9:17, 19, 31).

A Messianic Division

As I said previously, scholars who are working with the emerging new paradigm of "Israel and the Nations" see the change that occurs vis-à-vis Israel with the coming of Jesus as one that is not *away from* national Israel, but *within* national Israel. As has occurred many times in her history, Israel has now moved into a new "state" or "phase" or "mode of existence." Just as in times past she experienced deep divisions—(a) *politically*–as two nations under the Divided Monarchy (b) *geographically*–as a remnant in the land and those in the Diaspora at the time of The Return, and (c) *culturally/spiritually*–as a people deeply fractionated into various parties by the end of the Second Temple Period—so now, with the coming of her Messiah, something "unthinkable" occurs again. A significant portion of God's people reject the one presented to them as Messiah, son of David. As under the Divided Monarchy there was a majority of God's people who rejected a king of the Davidic line, so it happened at the time of Jesus. We could perhaps say that a major *Messianic*

---

179 Because of disobedience to the covenant, God at times threatens Israel with abandonment and even declares/predicts that he will do so: "And the Lord said to Moses, 'Behold, you are about to lie down with your fathers. Then this people will rise and whore after the foreign gods among them in the land that they are entering, and they will forsake me and break my covenant that I have made with them. Then my anger will be kindled against them in that day, and I will forsake them and hide my face from them, and they will be devoured. And many evils and troubles will come upon them, so that they will say in that day, "Have not these evils come upon us because our God is not among us?"'" (Deut. 31:16–17). But the abandonment is always temporal, not ultimate, e.g., "For a brief moment I deserted you, but with great compassion I will gather you" (Isa. 54:7).

division occurred among the people of God—a type of division that would repeat itself on other occasions in their subsequent history.[180]

It should be noted that this way of recounting history to remind the people of God of where they have been and what is required of them now is repeatedly used in the Tanakh.[181] And it was used by Jesus's Jewish followers, steeped in this tradition, to address their countrymen (Stephen in Acts 7:1–50 and Paul in Acts 13:16–23).

With this new change in her mode of existence, based on all prior changes, we should expect at least two things to obtain: (1) God will not forsake his people Israel, and (2) there will be a resulting change in her relationship to the Nations. And this is exactly what we find outlined in the pages of the NT!

The Two Portions of Israel in Messianic Times

The first thing we should expect to obtain, that God will not forsake his people, is stated clearly about both of the divisions in Israel. As to that portion that follows Jesus as Messiah, Paul makes it clear: "I ask, then, has God rejected his people? By no means! For I myself am an Israelite, a descendant of Abraham, a member of the tribe of Benjamin" (Rom. 11:1). He goes on to say that he is currently part of a remnant, just as there was in the days of Elijah (Rom. 11:2–5), and we might add, as in the days of the Divided Monarchy or in the Return from Babylonian exile. This, in itself, is nothing new.

But what about that larger portion of Israel that have not followed Jesus. Are they now cast off? Or, if that language sounds too harsh, do we embrace the mitigated idea that they no longer have a special place in the purposes of God and that they are just like everybody else among

180 See Kaufmann Kohler and H. G. Friedmann, "Pseudo-Messiahs," in the *Jewish Encyclopedia*, 1906, http://www.jewishencyclopedia.com/articles/12416-pseudo-messiahs (accessed Nov. 1, 2018).

181 "Reciting Israel's history in ways to make points was common (historical retrospective, e.g., 1 Samuel 12:7–12; 1 Macc. 2:49–69; Ecclus. 44–50)." Craig S. Keener, *The IVP Bible Background Commentary: NT* (Downers Grove, IL: InterVarsity Press, 1993), 339. See also Deut. 9:1–29 and Jer. 2:1–13.

the Nations? Disobedient Israel in times past was not cast off and the same is true with this manifestation of disobedience. Again, Paul's answer leaves no room for doubt or equivocation on this matter. He declares, "As regards the gospel, they are enemies for your sake. But as regards election, they are beloved for the sake of their forefathers. For the gifts and the calling of God are irrevocable" (Rom. 11:28–29). He is absolutely clear that he is talking about that part of Israel (the Jewish people) who have not embraced Jesus—"as regards the gospel, they are enemies." Yet he goes on to say of this very people that regarding their election or chosenness, they are still beloved for the sake of their forefathers, a reference to the covenant promises made to Abraham, Isaac, and Jacob (Deut. 10:15). And he concludes by saying that the gifts and calling of God are irrevocable.

God has not forsaken that portion of Israel that follows Jesus and he has not forsaken that portion of Israel that does not follow Jesus. But the ways in which he continues to stand with and deal with each is quite different! This brings us to the second thing, based on previous history, that we should expect to obtain with this new change that has occurred in Israel's mode of existence with the coming of her Messiah—there will be a resulting change in her relationship to the Nations. And again, this is, in fact, what we find.

All of the Jewish people will experience the devastation of their holy city and temple destroyed by the Nations (Rome and the various people groups who make up the empire). Furthermore, they will be scattered among the Nations as in the Babylonian Captivity, only this time it will be worldwide in scope.[182] Concerning that portion of Israel that *does not* embrace Jesus as her Messiah, Jesus predicted, "They will fall by the edge of the sword and be led captive among *all* nations, and Jerusalem will be trampled underfoot by the Gentiles, until the times of the Gentiles are fulfilled" (Luke 21:24). It is important to note the accuracy of the first part of the prediction as well as the subordinating conjunction

[182] Although the Jewish people en masse were dispersed worldwide, there has nonetheless been an unbroken presence of *some* Jewish people in the land of Promise since the time of Joshua!

until which introduces the second part, i.e., the devastation/occupation of Jerusalem by the Nations and the scattering of the people among the Nations has an end point—it is not permanent.[183]

Concerning that portion of Israel that *does* embrace Jesus as her Messiah, they will likewise experience a change in relationship to the Nations, but differently from their kinsman in at least two ways. The *first* difference is that rather than being forcibly scattered among all Nations, they are being sent:

> "Go therefore and make disciples of all nations..." (Matt. 28:19)
>
> "As the Father has sent me, even so I am sending you." (John 20:21)
>
> "For so the Lord has commanded us, saying, 'I have made you a light for the Gentiles, that you may bring salvation to the ends of the earth.'" (Acts 13:48, cf. Isa. 49:6)

GENTILES BECOME *PEOPLE OF GOD*

In their sojourn among the Nations, they will likewise experience persecution and hardship among the Nations just as their other brethren: "Then they will deliver you up to tribulation and put you to death, and you will be hated by all nations for my name's sake" (Matt. 24:9). But, there will also be another reaction among the Nations that, from the entire history of Israel's relationship with them is, in a word, "unthinkable." And this leads to the *second* difference in their experience of change in relationship to the Nations: Some individuals from among each of the Nations of the earth will receive their message about Israel's Messiah and become a part of the people of God! The Tanakh predicts re-

---

[183] Even in the times of most severe chastisement, when we might imagine that God has truly forsaken his people, he promises to be with them: "Therefore say, 'Thus says the Lord GOD: Though I removed them far off among the nations, and though I scattered them among the countries, yet I have been a sanctuary to them for a while in the countries where they have gone'" (Ezek. 11:16). While it may be argued that this promise had its fulfillment with the Babylonian Captivity, it may be counter-argued that the principle nonetheless holds and, in fact, this prophetic word may have multiple fulfillments as is not uncommon in the Tanakh.

peatedly that one day there would be "foreigners who join themselves to the Lord" (Isa. 56:6) and worship the God of Israel. At least two passages specifically declare that at some future time God will call people of the Nations "my people":

> In that day Israel will be the third with Egypt and Assyria, a blessing in the midst of the earth, whom the Lord of hosts has blessed, saying, "Blessed be Egypt **my people**, and Assyria the work of my hands, and Israel my inheritance." (Isa. 19:23–25)
>
> And many nations shall join themselves to the Lord in that day, and shall be **my people**. (Zech. 2:11)

That the Nations would one day turn to the Lord and be called his people was clearly declared in the Tanakh. But that it would happen in this way was not. Paul referred to this phenomenon as a *mystery*[184] that had not been revealed previously:

> For this reason I, Paul, a prisoner of Christ Jesus on behalf of you Gentiles—assuming that you have heard of the stewardship of God's grace that was given to me for you, how the mystery was made known to me by revelation, as I have written briefly. When you read this, you can perceive my insight into the mystery of Christ, which was not made known to the sons of men in other generations as it has now been revealed to his holy apostles and prophets by the Spirit. This mystery is that the Gentiles are fellow heirs, members of the same body, and partakers of the promise in Christ Jesus through the gospel. (Eph. 3:1–6)

The fact that God would do a "new thing" in Israel's history that had not been seen before or anticipated is nothing new! Who among the people of Israel could have imagined God opening a sea, or feeding them with manna, or living under the glory of Solomon, or dividing them into two kingdoms, or sending them into Babylonian captivity?

---

[184] For a definition of the use of this word in the NT, see the first chapter.

God even announces:

> "Behold, the former things have come to pass, and new things I now declare; before they spring forth I tell you of them." (Isa. 42:9)
>
> "Behold, I am doing a new thing; now it springs forth, do you not perceive it? I will make a way in the wilderness and rivers in the desert." (Isa. 43:19)
>
> "Look among the nations, and see; wonder and be astounded. For I am doing a work in your days that you would not believe if told." (Hab. 1:5)

Not only will God, on occasion, declare and do a new thing, there is also a question as to whether his people will perceive it and further, even believe it. While preaching to his countrymen, Paul quotes Habakkuk 1:5 and charges them with this very failure in their hour (Acts 13:41).

Gentiles Don't Become Israel

But if a large portion of Israel misunderstood the prophetic scriptures and what God was doing with them and their relationship to the Nations with the coming of Jesus, the ever-swelling ranks of Gentiles turning to Israel's Messiah soon misunderstood the implications of all that was happening as well. In spite of Paul's very clear warning to them to the contrary (Rom. 11:11–29), that they should not become arrogant and think that God was finished in his dealings with Israel, the leadership of the Gentile congregations in the Diaspora began to assert a simple but false equation: "The people God called 'my people' before the coming of Jesus were identified by the name *Israel.* With the coming of Jesus, God is now calling us Gentiles 'my people.' Therefore, *we* are now identified by the name *Israel*—not the Jews." This syllogism is exegetically unsustainable. With the exception of one controversial verse (Gal. 6:16), the NT consistently and clearly uses the word *Israel* to refer to the

Jewish people.[185] Furthermore, while phrases like "one new man" (Eph. 2:15) and "there is neither Jew nor Greek" (Gal. 3:28) or "For not all who are descended from Israel belong to Israel" (Rom. 9:6), in isolation, might lead one to believe that there is absolutely no longer any distinctions between Jewish people and those of the Nations within the body of Messiah, a more careful reading of these passages in their full context points rather to a unity in diversity.[186]

For example, in the passage quoted immediately above, Paul uses language that both indicates equality and unity as well as diversity—"fellow heirs, members of the same body, and partakers of the promise in Christ Jesus" (Eph. 3:6). The underlying Greek word translated here as *fellow heirs*[187] is the same word used in Romans 8:17 which speaks of believers as adopted children of God: "and if children, then heirs—heirs of God and *fellow heirs* with Christ." To my knowledge, no commentator has ever suggested that this means there is absolutely no differentiation or distinction between believers and Jesus. Rather, as F. F. Bruce explains: "They are joint-heirs with Christ because the glory which they will inherit by grace is the glory which is His by right (cf. Jn. 27:22–24)."[188] So Gentiles, those of the Nations who are joined to Israel's Messiah, have now become joint heirs along with the Jewish people of all the good things their Messiah has brought about. But these Gentiles

---

185 See chapter four under the heading: **A Future for the People of Israel**.

186 For example, Paul's statement in Galatians 3:28 that "There is neither Jew nor Greek, there is neither slave nor free, there is no male and female, for you are all one in Christ Jesus" is sometimes used as a "universal acid" to dissolve all distinctions within the body of Christ. Yet Paul goes on in several of his letters to talk about how men should conduct themselves, how women should conduct themselves, how slaves should conduct themselves, and how free men should conduct themselves. The Galatian 3:28 statement is referring to one's standing before God in Christ and the salvific benefits that flow therefrom. For elucidation on Rom. 9:6 see Eli Lizorkin-Eyzenberg, "Are Gentiles Stones Turned Children?" https://weekly.israelbiblecenter.com/gentiles-stones-turned-children/ (accessed Feb. 28, 2018).

187 συγκληρονόμος ὁ, ἡ, (sugkleronomos) a fellow-heir, a joint-heir: Romans 8:17; Ephesians 3:6; one who obtains something assigned to himself with others, a joint participant THAYER'S GREEK LEXICON, Electronic Database. Copyright © 2002, 2003, 2006, 2011 by Biblesoft, Inc. All rights reserved. Used by permission. BibleSoft.com.

188 F. F. Bruce, *The Epistle of Paul to the Romans*, in *The Tyndale NT Commentaries*, ed. R. V. G. Tasker (Grand Rapids, MI: Eerdmans Publishing Co., 1963, 1976), 167.

don't displace or replace Israel, rather, they join with that part of Israel that currently recognizes her Messiah. There is an *extending* of the promises originally made to Israel—not a *transfer*.

What I have said here about the phrase *fellow heirs* could, in a similar way, also be said about the phrase *members of the same body*. The same Paul who wrote that also wrote "But as it is, God arranged the members in the body, each one of them, as he chose. If all were a single member, where would the body be? As it is, there are many parts, yet one body" (1 Cor. 12:18–20). While here Paul was talking about the diversity of gifts and ministries (members) in one church (body), the power of the analogy demonstrating diversity in unity is the same.

If I may add my own analogy here, I would say that God does not dump Jewish people and Gentiles into a blender, turn it on, and make an undifferentiated, homogeneous lump which will now be called "the new humanity" or "the new race." Rather, as George Howard asserts:

> The gospel as Paul preached it demanded a continued ethnic distinctiveness between Jews and Gentiles in order that . . . [Adonai], the God of the Hebrews, could be conceptualized by both Jews and Gentiles as the God of all nations. . . . This is certainly his point of view in Rom. 3:29–30 where he says: "Or is God the God of the Jews only? Is he not the God of the Gentiles also? Yes, of the Gentiles also, since God is one." His thought is: If God is one he must be the God of both Jews and Gentiles. . . . We may even go further and say that any attempt on either side to erase the ethnic and cultural nature of the other would be to destroy Paul's particular concept of unity between Jews and Gentiles.[189]

Since God is the God of the Gentiles/Nations, the people of the Nations do not have to become Jewish in order for God to be their God. In fact, they should *not* become Jewish because then there would be no more Nations—entities which God created to display his glory in multi-

[189] George Howard, *Paul: Crisis in Galatia: A Study in Early Christian Theology* (Richmond, VA: John Knox, 1969), 90–91; cited in *Introduction to Messianic Judaism*, 14.

faceted ways alongside Israel. David Rudolph relates this helpful insight to the discussion: "Countering Paul van Buren's argument that 'Only one Jew is essential to the Church and that is the Jew Jesus,' Isaac Rottenburg points out that 'Jewish-Gentile unity belongs to the *esse* [being], not just the *bene esse* [well-being] of the Church.'"[190] And R. Kendall Soulen adds:

> Traditionally, the church has understood itself as a spiritual fellowship in which the carnal distinction between Jew and Gentile no longer applies. The church has declared itself a third and final 'race' that transcends and replaces the difference between Israel and the nations. . . . The proper therapy for this misunderstanding is a recovery of the church's basic character as a table fellowship of those who are—and remain—different. The distinction between Jew and Gentile, being intrinsic to God's work as the Consummator of creation, is not erased but realized in a new way in the sphere of the church. The church concerns the Jew as a Jew and the Gentile as a Gentile, not only initially or for the period of a few generations but essentially and at all times."[191]

Further reinforcing this idea of continued Jewish–Gentile distinctions within unity, it is also important to observe that within his letters, Paul is most often talking to all believers, both Jewish and Gentile, without distinction. But at other times he addresses one group or another. For examples, as in the Ephesian passage above, he specifically addresses the Gentiles in Ephesians 3:1: "For this reason I, Paul, a prisoner of Christ Jesus on behalf of you Gentiles—assuming that you have heard of the stewardship of God's grace that was given to me for you." The same is true in Romans 11:13: "Now I am speaking to you Gentiles . . . " But in Romans 3, he specifically addresses his fellow Jewish followers of Jesus: "Then what advantage has the Jew? Or what is the val-

---

190 Ibid., 14–15. Paul M. van Buren, *Discerning the Way* (New York, NY: Seabury, 1980), 155; Isaac C. Rottenburg, *Jewish Christians in an Age of Christian-Jewish Dialogue* (1995), 99;

191 R. Kendall Soulen, *The God of Israel and Christian Theology* (Minneapolis, MN: Fortress Press, 1996), 169–170.

ue of circumcision? Much in every way. To begin with, the Jews were entrusted with the oracles of God. . . . What then? Are we Jews any better off? No, not at all. For we have already charged that all, both Jews and Greeks, are under sin . . ." (Rom. 3:1–2, 9–10).

Finally, a very important but often overlooked passage germane to this discussion is 1 Corinthians 7:17–20:

> "Only let each person lead the life that the Lord has assigned to him, and to which God has called him. **This is my rule in all the churches**. Was anyone at the time of his call already circumcised? Let him not seek to remove the marks of circumcision. Was anyone at the time of his call uncircumcised? Let him not seek circumcision. For neither circumcision counts for anything nor uncircumcision, but keeping the commandments of God. **Each one should remain in the condition in which he was called.**"

It is a rule, not merely a custom, that Gentiles should not try to become Jews and Jews should not try to become Gentiles. There is not to be a "homogenizing" of that which the Lord had *assigned.* Gentiles should remain in the condition in which they were called. They have been called into Messiah Jesus to fulfill an assignment. The same is true for the Jewish people called into Messiah. They are not to abandon the assignment to which they have also been called. Simply stated, Gentiles individually do not become Jews and corporately do not become Israel.

Pacification of the Nations

The point is, from a fully biblical perspective, one cannot make Jesus into some sort of non-ethnic, cosmic Christ who brings "spiritual (i.e., non-material) salvation" to a non-ethnic, indistinguishable, generic humanity. Rather, concerning Christ: "the particularity of Jewish flesh crosses the threshold into the eternal state."[192] Jesus is Jewish and came

[192] Rudolph, *Introduction to Messianic Judaism,* 253.

to establish God's promises to Israel, the Jewish people.[193] And in order to do that, he also has to do something with the Nations. This is very difficult to talk about because the vast history of antisemitism and persecution of the Jewish people by the institutional church testifies against what I am about to say.[194] But getting back to "beginning with the end in mind," if there are going to be Nations at peace with Israel at the end of history, they have to be pacified and reconciled to Israel and, therefore, Israel's God. Unless we want to say that God will (forgive the crudity of the illustration) shove his arm down their collective throats and turn their hearts to be like a robot and say, "God, I love you; Israel, I love you," he will have to do something else. If he immediately sends a Messiah in the mold of a Judah Maccabee, he might kill most of Israel's enemies and subdue the rest, but it is hard to imagine them not seething in resentment against Israel and Israel's God. Certainly not the best conditions for peace and sincere worship and certainly not what is depicted by the prophets.

In his letter to the Ephesians, Paul argues that God has found a way to pacify the Gentiles without resorting to these untenable measures:

> But now in Christ Jesus you who once were far off have been brought near by the blood of Christ. For he himself is our peace, who has made us both one and has broken down in his flesh the dividing wall of hostility by abolishing the law of commandments expressed in ordinances, that he might create in himself one new man in place of the two, so making peace, and might reconcile us both to God in one body through the cross, thereby killing the hostility. (Eph. 2:13–16)

In stark contrast to the antisemitism displayed by the leaders of the in-

---

[193] Paul's statement in Romans 15:8 – 9 is exactly on point: "For I tell you that Christ became a servant to the circumcised to show God's truthfulness, in order to confirm the promises given to the patriarchs, and in order that the Gentiles might glorify God for his mercy. As it is written, 'Therefore I will praise you among the Gentiles, and sing to your name.'"

[194] For two examples among many good works on this topic see Flannery, *The Anguish of the Jews*, 1985); and for a more popular treatment by a scholar see Michael L. Brown, *Our Hands Are Stained with Blood: The Tragic Story of the "Church" and the Jewish People* (Shippensburg, PA: Destiny Image Publications, Inc., 1992).

stitutional church from the second century on, there have always been followers of Jesus from among the Nations who have been so transformed by their relationship with him that they have shown an extraordinary love for the Jewish people—even to the point of laying down their lives for them. And I am happy to report that there is a vast multitude of people from every ethnic group in the world, growing exponentially daily, that are coming into a living relationship with the God of Israel through *this* Jesus (there is *another* Jesus, cf. 2 Cor. 11:3), and in so doing they are coming into a love and respect for the Jewish people and the land of Israel.

Church as Prolepsis of Israel and the Nations

Jesus said, "I will build ***my*** *congregation-ekklesia-called out assembly-church*," made up of people from Israel and people from the Nations who listen to his words. This congregation/church is not called Israel—but neither is it something totally different from Israel. It is the name given to a growing group of people who will ultimately fulfill God's declared purposes that "the earth shall be filled with the knowledge of the glory of the LORD as the waters cover the sea" (Hab. 2:14) as "Israel and the Nations" dwell together in *shalom*. They form in this present age a model, a proto-type, a prophetic picture, of what the future will hold. As David Rudolph puts it, "the church is a prolepsis[195] of 'Israel and the Nations' in the eschaton [the final event in the divine plan; the end of the world]. Interdependence and mutual blessing between Jew and Gentile reflect the raison d'être of the church and anticipate the consummation when Israel and the nations, in unity and diversity, will worship Adonai alone."[196] Douglas Harink elaborates:

> There is no New Testament theological reason to think that the cor-

[195] "The representation or assumption of a future act or development as if presently existing or accomplished." Miriam-Webster Dictionary, "prolepsis," https://www.merriam-webster.com/dictionary/prolepsis (accessed Nov. 14, 2018).

[196] David Rudolph, *Introduction to Messianic Judaism,* 14.

porate, theo-political vision of the Hebrew Scriptures for Israel and the nations comes to an end with the coming of Jesus. Rather, that vision is both intensified in and for Israel and announced as the true destiny of the Gentile nations in the Messiah. The sign, witness, sacrament, and down payment of that vision is the table fellowship and worship of Jews and Gentiles together in the messianic theo-political reality called the *ekklesia* — where Jews as Jews practice Torah, the *telos* of which is given in the Messiah, and Gentiles as Gentiles work out their own salvation in fear and trembling in the Messiah; where each group gives itself in cruciform service, indeed sacrifice, for the sake of the other; where each group seeks to build the other up in its unique form of witness; where each group displays toward its wider theo-political body of origin, whether Israel or the nations, a testimony to the cruciform way of the Messiah in this time before the time of the restoration of all things and of the kingdom to Israel; where each group seeks blessing and to be a blessing in the midst of these wider theo-political realities for their welfare and healing. Precisely as sign, witness, sacrament, and down payment, the *ekklesia* in its ongoing duality as messianic Jews and messianic Gentiles anticipates, hopes, and prays for the full theo-political reality of Israel and the nations living at peace under the reign of Jesus the Messiah.[197]

CONTINUITIES AND DISCONTINUITIES

In this chapter, the primary train of thought has been on those portions of Scripture which emphasize the *continuities* between God's dealings with "Israel and the Nations" in the past and what he was and is now doing with them through the coming of Jesus. But it is also very clear that with the coming of Jesus, there are also *discontinuities* with what God has done in the past and what he is doing now. I have already alluded to this dynamic of God doing "a new thing" in the subsection above titled GENTILES BECOME *PEOPLE OF GOD*. To be clear, that the coming Messiah/Deliverer would in some way be divine was, in fact, not alien to

[197] Douglas Harink, "Jewish Priority, Election, and the Gospel," in *Introduction to Messianic Judaism*, 279.

the faith of Israel in the second temple period.[198] Likewise, that a messianic figure would somehow die for his people was anticipated.[199] But that this Messiah would die for the sins of his people, be buried, and rise again from the dead on the third day, although supported by the Tanakh when read *retrospectively* in the light of these realities,[200] could not have been, and in fact, was not *anticipated.* This was clearly an "unthinkable" new thing that God had done! And if this messianic trajectory of death-burial-resurrection could not have been conceived by the faithful in Israel prior to its realization, what it would fully achieve was totally opaque to them. I am here referring to those Levitical and temple practices which, in the light of the advent of the Messiah, are viewed in the NT as foreshadowing all that he would accomplish.[201] This *all* would include but not be limited to:

- *Atonement* – at-one-ment with God and man
- *Justification* – right standing with God

---

198 Daniel Boyarin, a modern orthodox Jewish Talmudic scholar states: "There is significant evidence that in the first century many—perhaps most—Jews held to a binitarian doctrine of God." Daniel, Boyarin, *Borderlines: The Partition of Judaeo-Christianity* (Phila., PA: Univ. of Penn. Press, 2004), 131. See all of Chapter 5 in this work, "The Jewish Life of the Logos: Logos Theology in Pre- and Pararabbinic Judaism" for a full discussion of the topic. See also Messianic Jewish scholar Michael L. Brown, *Answering Jewish Objections to Jesus: Volume Two—Theological Objections* (Grand Rapids, MI: Baker Books, 2000), 3–48; 211–220. On page 211 Brown points out that "John Collins, a widely respected specialist in apocalyptic literature, notes that rather than thinking of first-century C.E. Jewish belief in either an earthly Messiah or a heavenly Messiah, 'we should think of a spectrum of messianic expectation, ranging from the earthly messiah of the Psalms of Solomon and several Dead Sea Scrolls, through the transcendent messiah of 4 Ezra to the heavenly figure of the Similitudes of Enoch.'" John Collins, *The Scepter and the Star: Messianism in Light of the Dead Sea Scrolls* (Grand Rapids, MI: Eerdmans, 1994), 189.

199 J. Immanuel Schochet, "Moshiach 101," in Appendix II on the Chabad.org website (accessed Nov. 28, 2018) https://www.chabad.org/library/article_cdo/aid/101747/jewish/Appendix-II.htm. See also Brown above in the subsection 3:23 "Jews don't believe in a suffering Messiah," 221–231.

200 "Now I would remind you, brothers, of the gospel I preached to you. . . . For I delivered to you as of first importance what I also received: that Christ died for our sins in accordance with the Scriptures, that he was buried, that he was raised on the third day in accordance with the Scriptures" (1 Cor. 15:1, 3–4). See Michael L. Brown, *Answering Jewish Objections to Jesus: Volume Three—Messianic Prophecy Objections* (Grand Rapids, MI: Baker Books, 2003).

201 These can be found in any good textbook on systematic theology. Two that I have used with benefit to my students are Millard J. Erickson, *Christian Theology* (Grand Rapids, MI: Baker Books, 1983, 1998) and Wayne Grudem, *Systematic Theology: An Introduction to Biblical Doctrine* (Grand Rapids, MI: Zondervan Publishing House, 1994).

- *Sanctification* – being set apart with a view toward holiness
- *Cleansing* – from sin's defilement and guilt
- *Redemption* – bought back from the dominions of death and the powers of the evil one
- *Empowerment* – indwelt by the Holy Spirt to overcome the enticements of the world, the flesh, and the devil and gifted to serve God and humanity
- *Identification* – to be placed *in Christ*; a phrase repeatedly used that incorporates all of the previous benefits listed and yet also transcends them

It is perhaps because of all of these *unexpected*, *discontinuous*, and outstanding blessings that the Messiah accomplished under the subheading ***Cross***, that the *expected, continuous* part of the Big Story, of God's dealings with "Israel and the Nations," got sublimated or lost.

Part of what the priests were upset about was that Jesus called himself God? Caiaphas tore his shirt in half.

NINE

The Rest of the Story: *Consummation*

We have now come to the final *C* in our summary of The Big Story and that is ***C**onsummation.* Much of which needs to be said here has already been set forth in chapter five. As we "keep the end in mind" we recognize that there is going to come a "time for restoring all the things about which God spoke by the mouth of his holy prophets long ago" (Acts 3:21) on a renewed earth. And central to the "all the things" to be restored of which the prophets spoke repeatedly are "Israel and the Nations"—which restoration has already begun in the *ekklesia* of the Messiah and is the proleptic guarantee of its fulfillment.

The Millennial Question

As we talk about the consummation of all things, inevitably the question of the Millennium arises. Since this subject has already been referenced by several different authors I have cited throughout this treatise, I will only add here a very insightful quote from Randy Alcorn as to how I think we should handle this thorny issue with regard to "Israel and the Nations":

> Though I don't believe the case for postmillennialism is strong (either biblically or in light of human history), both premillennialism and amillennialism have many biblical points in their favor. I personally believe there will be a literal thousand-year reign of Christ on the present

> Earth (though I'm not dogmatic on this point), but I also understand and respect the strong interpretive arguments that have been made in support of amillennialism.
>
> Although the Millennium is a subject of interest to many, it's not the subject of this book [*Heaven*]. I mention it only to point out that our beliefs about the Millennium need not affect our view of the New Earth. The Millennium question relates to whether the old Earth will end after the return of Christ or a thousand years later after the end of the Millennium. But regardless of when the old Earth ends, the central fact is that *the New Earth will begin.* The Bible is emphatic that God's ultimate Kingdom and our final home will *not* be on the old Earth but on the New Earth, where at last God's original design will be fulfilled and enjoyed *forever—not* just for a thousand years. Hence, no matter how differently we may view the Millennium, we can still embrace a common theology of the New Earth.[202]

I completely agree with Alcorn that "our beliefs about the Millennium need not affect our view of the New Earth." And since "Israel and the Nations" are part of God's good creation that he is going to restore in the New Earth, our view of their ultimate destinies need not be affected by our millennial views.

ALL ISRAEL SAVED

Recognizing that entire books have been written on the subject of eschatology (the study of "last things"), I must confine our summary of ***C**onsummation* to one final point of inquiry: How will Israel stand *primus*

---

[202] Alcorn, *Heaven*, 146. He also makes this insightful comment: "Throughout church history, some Bible students have believed that the thousand-year kingdom spoken of in Revelation 20 is literal. Others believe it is figurative. I cannot resolve that debate. My point here is not to say that Isaiah 60 and 65 don't refer to a literal thousand-year reign of Christ on the old Earth. Rather, I am saying that they do refer to the eternal reign of Christ on the New Earth. It is common for prophetic statements to have partial fulfillment in one era and complete fulfillment in another. It may be that these passages will have a partial and initial fulfillment in a literal millennium, explaining why the passages contain a few allusions to death, which is incompatible with the New Earth. But, in context, these prophecies go far beyond a temporary kingdom on an Earth that is still infected by sin, curse, and death, and that ends with judgment and destruction. They speak of an eternal kingdom, a messianic reign over a renewed Earth that lasts forever, on which sin, curse, and death have no place at all" (147–148).

inter pares (first among equals) with the Nations in a restored earth under the loving rulership of Jesus if the Jewish people, for the larger part, have not yet acknowledged him as their Messiah?

Again, this is a very difficult subject to talk about because of the shameful history of the institutional church with its blatant displays of antisemitism (see all of chapter three) and forced "conversions." So it is incumbent upon me as a non-Jewish writer to present this as carefully and, if I may put it this way, as "Jewishly" as I can.

Paul declares unequivocally that "all Israel will be saved" (Rom. 11:26), a conviction also held by Rabbinic Judaism.[203] Commentators generally agree that this does not mean every single Jewish person will attain salvation, but rather Israel, i.e., the Jewish people as a whole.[204] How will this come about? Paul explains using the metaphor of an olive tree and its branches.

> If the dough offered as firstfruits is holy, so is the whole lump, and if the root is holy, so are the branches. But if some of the branches were broken off, and you [Gentiles], although a wild olive shoot, were grafted in among the others and now share in the nourishing root of the olive tree, do not be arrogant toward the branches. If you are, remember it is not you who support the root, but the root that supports you. Then you will say, "Branches were broken off so that I might be grafted in." That is true. They were broken off because of their unbelief, but you stand fast through faith. So do not become proud, but fear. For if God did not spare the natural branches, neither will he spare you. Note then the kindness and the severity of God: severity toward those who have fallen, but God's kindness to you, provided you continue in his kindness. Otherwise you too will be cut off. And even they, if they do not continue in their unbelief, will be grafted in,

203 Jacob Neusner, "All Israel Has A Portion In The World To Come," in *The Talmud: Law, Theology, Narrative: A Sourcebook – Studies in Judaism* (Lanham, MD: Univ. Press of America, Inc., 2005), 109–119. It is interesting to note that after this unequivocal declaration about the destiny of "all Israel," the Talmud goes on to list various kinds of Jewish individuals who will not share this destiny. It also declares that the righteous among the Gentiles shall also have a portion in the world to come (109 ff.).

204 For an elaboration see Craig Keener, "Interdependence and Mutual Blessing in the Church," in *Introduction to Messianic Judaism,* 192.

> for God has the power to graft them in again. For if you were cut from what is by nature a wild olive tree, and grafted, contrary to nature, into a cultivated olive tree, how much more will these, the natural branches, be grafted back into their own olive tree. (Rom. 11:16–24)

So much could be said here, but for the moment we will observe that Paul is making the case in the strongest way possible that this Jesus/Yeshua messianic faith is intimately connected with "the olive tree," the perennial symbol of Israel.[205] He is not alone in asserting the primacy of messianic faith for the Jewish people. The Talmud declares that *"All the prophets prophesied not but of the days of the Messiah"* (Sanhedrin 99a) and Maimonides "Thirteen Principles of Faith" includes, "I believe with complete faith in the coming of Moshiach, and although he may tarry, nevertheless, I wait every day for him to come."[206] So there cannot be anything more Jewish, more natural, than for Jewish people to believe in

---

205 "More than once the prophets had pictured the nation of Israel as the olive tree of God. That was natural, because the olive tree was the commonest and most useful tree in the Mediterranean world. 'The Lord once called you a green olive tree, fair with goodly fruit' (Jeremiah 11:16). 'His shoots shall spread out; his beauty shall be like the olive'" (Hosea 14:6). William Barclay, "The Letter to the Romans," in *The Daily Bible Study Series* (Philadelphia, PA: The Westminster Press, 1975), 176. "Our parsha begins with the words: 'Command the Israelites to bring you clear olive oil, crushed for the light, so that the lamp may always burn' (Ex. 27:20). The sages drew a comparison between the olive and the Jewish people. 'Rabbi Joshua ben Levi asked, why is Israel compared to an olive? Just as an olive is first bitter, then sweet, so Israel suffers in the present but great good is stored up for them in the time to come. And just as the olive only yields its oil by being crushed – as it is written, clear olive oil, crushed for the light – so Israel fulfils [its full potential in] the Torah only when it is pressed by suffering.' Midrash Pitron Torah to Num. 13:2." Jonathan Sacks, *"Crushed for the Light,"* Tetzaveh 5778, Covenant and Conversation, Life Changing Ideas in the Parsha, http://rabbisacks.org/crushed-light-tetzaveh-5778/ (accessed Feb. 21, 2018).

206 "The great codifier of Torah law and Jewish philosophy, Rabbi Moshe ben Maimon ('*Maimonides*' also known as 'The *Rambam*' [1135–1204]), compiled what he refers to as the Shloshah Asar Ikkarim, the 'Thirteen Fundamental Principles' of the Jewish faith, as derived from the Torah. Maimonides refers to these thirteen principles of faith as 'the fundamental truths of our religion and its very foundations' ... It is the custom of many congregations to recite the Thirteen Articles, in a slightly more poetic form, beginning with the words Ani Maamin—'I believe'—every day after the morning prayers in the synagogue." Chabad.org, "The Thirteen Principles of Jewish Faith," https://www.chabad.org/library/article_cdo/aid/332555/jewish/Maimonides-13-Principles-of-Faith.htm (accessed Dec. 8, 2018). The Jews For Judaism website gives the more complete rendering: 12. "I believe with complete faith in the coming of Moshiach, and although he may tarry, nevertheless, I wait every day for him to come." Jews For Judaism, "13 Principles of Faith," https://jewsforjudaism.org/knowledge/articles/13-principles-of-faith/ (accessed Dec. 8, 2018).

their promised Messiah—for "the natural branches [to] be grafted back into *their own* olive tree." What is actually "unnatural" is for peoples of the Nations to believe in the Jewish Messiah—to be "grafted, contrary to nature, into a cultivated olive tree."[207]

Of course, the multi-trillion-dollar question is the identity of the Messiah. A wonderful quip, popular in Jewish-Christian dialogue circles and attributed to the Jewish philosopher Martin Buber, goes "…when He [the Messiah] will come, we will ask Him, have you been here before?"[208] If the answer is "Yes," it will not be an occasion for Gentile gloating. If Jesus/Yeshua turns out to be the Jewish messiah, Gentiles who had believed in him will not taunt those Jewish people who had not by chanting like little children "Nyah nyah nyah nyah nyah nyah,[209] we were right and you were wrong." Rather, it will be something like the incredible moment when a very Egyptian/Gentile/Person-of-the-Nations looking Joseph revealed himself in a sacred, private moment to his brothers and spoke to them in their own language (Gen. 45:1–14).

---

[207] "So Paul thinks of the Gentiles as branches of wild olive engrafted into the garden olive tree which was Israel. From the point of view of horticulture Paul's picture is impossible. In horticulture it is the good olive that is grafted into the stock of the wild olive so that a fruit-bearing olive may result. The process that Paul pictures was never used in actual practice, because it would have served no useful purpose. But the point Paul wishes to make is quite clear. The Gentiles had been out in the deserts and the wildernesses and among the wild briars; and now, by the act of God's grace, they are engrafted into the richness and fertility of the garden olive tree." Barclay, "The Letter to the Romans," 176–177.

[208] Author Alan Brill on his blogsite asserts that the quote is probably one made up by Elie Wiesel: "Elie Wiesel is known for making up his own Hasidic tales to fit his ideas of arguing with God … But it seems Wiesel has also applied his craft of memoir (he rejects the label novelist) directly to Martin Buber. Here is the full quote: 'My good friends, what is the difference between you and me? Both of us, all of us believe, because we are religious, in the coming of the Messiah. You believe that the Messiah came, went back, and that you are waiting for Him for the second coming. We Jews believe He hasn't come yet, but He will come. In other words, we are waiting. You for the second coming, we for the first coming. Let's wait together.' After a pause, he said, 'And when He will come, we will ask Him, have you been here before?' Said Buber, 'I hope I will be behind Him and I will whisper in His ear, please do not answer.'" Elie Wiesel, *All Rivers Run to the Sea: Memoirs* (New York: Knopf, 1995), 354–55, on Alan Brill's blogsite: https://kavvanah.wordpress.com/2011/03/21/martin-buber-elie-wiesel-and-the-jewish-christian-encounter/ (accessed Dec. 10, 2018).

[209] The lexigraphic representation of a common children's chant. It is a rendering of one common vocalization for a six-note musical figure which is associated with children, is found in many European-derived cultures and is often used in taunting. Wikipedia, https://en.wikipedia.org/wiki/Nyah_nyah_nyah_nyah_nyah_nyah (accessed Dec. 11, 2018).

Paul does not describe this moment of recognition as "conversion." Rather, he describes it as coming into "fullness" (Rom. 11:12). They will not "convert to" or "join" an expression of the institutional church—Roman Catholic, Eastern Orthodox, Mainline Protestant, or evangelical. Rather, they will be joined to Yeshua and all of their Jewish brethren of the believing remnant, past and present, to stand together as redeemed Israel in the midst of redeemed Nations in fulfillment of the ancient promises made to Abraham and repeatedly reinforced by the prophets.

What I have just related is not mere prophetic speculation. The surety[210] of its full realization is already being demonstrated in our times as an increasing number of sabras,[211] whose "Jewishness" is beyond question—they speak and read Hebrew more fluently than most rabbis in the Diaspora and have served in the IDF—have also recognized Yeshua as the Messiah. Likewise, hundreds of thousands of Jewish people in the Diaspora have not only made the same discovery, but have done so in a way so as to preserve and strengthen their Jewish identities.[212] These together represent a continuity with that earlier remnant of Israel from the first few centuries who followed Yeshua yet fully kept their Jewish identity. They would describe their experience, not as "conversion," but as "teshuvah,"—a *return* to their roots in the Olive Tree.

---

210 Paul supports his teaching of a future for Israel with two illustrations, the batch of dough (v. 16) and the olive tree (vv. 16–24). Both demonstrate that God's past and present dealings with that people are the assurance of his future work on their behalf. The "part of the dough offered as firstfruits" [Numbers 15:17–21], which makes the "whole batch . . . holy," is probably a reference to the believing Jews (cf. Paul's use of "firstfruits" in 16:5 and 1 Cor. 16:15 for first converts). This present remnant of Jewish Christians, Paul says, represents the entire people and guarantees the final sanctification of the nation as a whole....However, the view of many that the firstfruits is a reference to the patriarchs, on the grounds that this must have the same meaning as "the root" in the same verse, would not negate the point of the illustration concerning the inclusion finally of the whole of Israel. Saucy, *Progressive Dispensationalism,* 251.

211 Sabra: a Jewish person born in Israel.

212 Due to the influences of secularism, inter-marriage, assimilation, and the devastations of the Holocaust, the majority of Jewish people in the world would consider themselves secular rather than religious. Jewish movements like Chabad have worked worldwide to bring Jewish individuals back to their ancient faith with some success, though not without some controversy due to messianic claims made about its founder Rabbi Menachem Mendel Schneerson. With some irony, the same might be said about the whole movement known as Messianic Judaism.

They have also come to acknowledge and deeply appreciate, and primarily through them a rapidly growing minority of Jesus-followers from the Nations, that this could not have happened without the faithfulness of that portion of Israel which did not follow Jesus. The rabbinic insistence on faithfulness to the Torah as practically expressed in Halakah,[213] kept the Jewish people and "Jewishness" alive in the earth, against the ravages of every kind of unimaginable persecution through the centuries—Christian, Muslim, and Secular. Without this faithfulness to the God of their fathers, however imperfectly understood or carried out, there would be no Jewish people in the earth and therefore, no possibility of the prophets' visions of a New Heaven and a New Earth with "Israel and the Nations" dwelling in shalom coming into realization. Further, these of "Israel and the Nations" who make up the *ekklesia* of Yeshua/Jesus have discovered in the rabbinic writings faith-enhancing riches of understanding and insight mined from thousands of years of meditation upon God's revelation in the Tanakh.

THE CONCLUSION OF THE FIVE *C'S*

This brings us to the conclusion of the five C's of the Big Story of the Bible: ***C**reation, **C**urse, **C**ovenant, **C**ross,* and ***C**onsummation.* I wish I could say with Paul Harvey, "And now you know—the rest of the story!" But Holy Writ cautions us to remember that now "we know in part" (1 Cor. 13:9). However, we are also encouraged by the same source that "the path of the righteous is like the light of dawn, which shines brighter and brighter until full day" (Prov. 4:18). With humble gratitude for all who have gone before us in wrestling with the Scriptures to bring us to this

---

213 "*Halakha* is the collective body of Jewish religious laws derived from the Written and Oral Torah. Halakha is based on biblical laws or 'commandments' (*mitzvot*) (traditionally numbered as 613), subsequent Talmudic and rabbinic law, and the customs and traditions compiled in the many books, one of the most famous of which is the 16th-century *Shulchan Aruch* (literally 'Prepared Table')." Wikipedia, "Halakha," https://en.wikipedia.org/wiki/Halakha (accessed Dec. 13, 2018). For a rich, scholarly description of and apologetic for the Halakhic way of life see Joseph B. Soloveitchik, *Halakhic Man* ((Philadelphia, PA: The Jewish Publication Society, 1983).

clearer place of understanding, may we all continue to "press on to know the LORD" (Hos. 6:3) and his purposes for "Israel and the Nations" contained in the mystery of *Jesus and the Olive Tree.*

EPILOGUE

PROLEPTICISM

Whenever I have had the opportunity to share some of the ideas presented in this book, frequently someone will ask, "So what is *this* view called? Historically, systematic theologians have given one-word labels such as Supersesssionism and Dispensationalism to these constructs of the Big Story of the Bible. Currently, I am not aware of any commonly used and definitively agreed upon term.

I like David Rudolph's use of the word *prolepsis:* "... the church is a prolepsis[214] of 'Israel and the Nations' in the eschaton [the final event in the divine plan; the end of the world]. Interdependence and mutual blessing between Jew and Gentile reflect the raison d'être of the church and anticipate the consummation when Israel and the nations, in unity and diversity, will worship Adonai alone."[215] (see page 97). I would be hard pressed to find a better, more concise description of this view of the grand narrative of the Bible.

So I would like to nominate *Prolepticism* as a worthy candidate for a one-word theological term to represent this understanding of God's

---

[214] Prolepsis (n.) 1570s, "the taking of something anticipated as already done or existing," from Latin prolepsis, from Greek prolepsis "an anticipating," literally "a taking beforehand," from prolambanein "to take before," from pro "before" (see pro-) + lambanein "to take" (see lemma). Related: Proleptic; proleptical; proleptically. – from the Online Etymology Dictionary, https://www.etymonline.com/ word/prolepsis (accessed Nov. 14, 2018).

[215] See footnote in chapter 8 in the subsection **Church as Prolepsis of Israel and the Nations.**

purposes. Granted, it's clunky and at first you don't know what it means. But the same charges could be made against Supersessionism and Dispensationalism—not to mention other theological terms such as *Supralapsarianism* (sorry, no footnote for that one)! One needs to learn what the terms mean, but once that is accomplished, they each provide an easy one-word way to refer to an entire body of thought. It strikes me that *Prolepticism* could serve that purpose for this emerging biblical paradigm as it denotatively captures some of the "already/not yet," "presence of the future" dynamics of the kingdom of God vis-à-vis "Israel and the Nations." It has the further benefit of not having been overly used.[216] So I will be using this term until my academic betters "show [me] a still more excellent way" (1 Cor. 12:31).

216 A brief Google search of *Prolepticism* showed only one use in a book title: Lauri T. Jäntti, *Prolepticism: The Futurist Theology of Ted Peters* (Helsinki, Finland: Luther-Agricola Society, 2017). Of course, the terms *prolepsis* and *proleptic* have been used to some extent in theological circles for a while, not to mention in literary and other fields of endeavor.

APPENDIX

This is a partial list of theologians cited in Randy Alcorn's book *Heaven*[217] who support the concept of God redeeming and restoring his original creation. The authors are listed in roughly the chronological order in which they lived or their works were published. The page numbers on which they are referenced appear in parentheses:

> "Heaven, as the eternal home of the divine Man and of all the redeemed members of the human race, must necessarily be thoroughly human in its structure, conditions, and activities. Its joys and activities must all be rational, moral, emotional, voluntary and active. There must be the exercise of all the faculties, the gratification of all tastes, the development of all talent capacities, the realization of all ideals. The reason, the intellectual curiosity, the imagination, the aesthetic instincts, the holy affections, the social affinities, the inexhaustible resources of strength and power native to the human must find in heaven exercise and satisfaction. Then there must always be a goal of endeavor before us, ever future. . . . Heaven will prove the consummate flower and fruit of the whole creation and of all the history of the universe." – *A. A. Hodge (98–99)*

> "God's honor consists precisely in the fact that he redeems and renews the same humanity, the same world, the same Heaven, and the same earth that have been corrupted and polluted by sin. Just as anyone in Christ is a new creation in whom the old has passed away and everything has become new (2 Corinthians 5:17), so this world passes away in its present form as well, in order out of its womb, at God's word of power, to give birth and being to a new world. . . . the rebirth of humans is completed in the rebirth of creation. The kingdom of God is fully realized only when it is visibly extended over the earth as well." – *Herman Bavinck (115)*

---

[217] Randy Alcorn, *Heaven* (Carol Stream, IL: Tyndale House Publishers, 2004).

"We will not be disembodied spirits in the world to come, but redeemed spirits, in redeemed bodies, in a redeemed universe." – *R. A. Torrey (112)*

"The hills and valleys of Heaven will be to those you now experience not as a copy is to an original, not as a substitute is to the genuine article, but as the flower to the root, or the diamond to the coal." – *C. S. Lewis (54)*

"Everything will be glorified, even nature itself. And that seems to me to be the biblical teaching about the eternal state: that what we call heaven is life in this perfect world as God intended humanity to live it. When he put Adam in Paradise at the beginning, Adam fell, and all fell with him, but men and women are meant to live in the body, and will live in a glorified body in a glorified world, and God will be with them." – *Martyn Lloyd-Jones (101)*

"The 'new Jerusalem' . . . does not remain in a 'heaven' far off in space, but it comes down to the renewed earth; there the redeemed will spend eternity in resurrection bodies. So heaven and earth, now separated, will then be merged: the new earth will also be heaven, since God will dwell there with his people. Glorified believers, in other words, will continue to be in heaven while they are inhabiting the new earth." – *Anthony Hoekema (45)*

"Christians often talk about living with God 'in heaven' forever. But in fact the biblical teaching is richer than that: it tells us that there will be new heavens and a new earth—an entirely renewed creation—and we will live with God there. . . . There will also be a new kind of unification of heaven and earth. . . . There will be a joining of heaven and earth in this new creation." – *Wayne Grudem (42)*

"What happens to our bodies and what happens to the creation go together. And what happens to our bodies is not annihilation but redemption. . . . Our bodies will be redeemed, restored, made new, not thrown way. And so it is with the heavens and the earth" – *John Piper (131)*

"The life we now have as the persons we now are will continue in the universe in which we now exist." – *Dallas Willard (159)*

ACKNOWLEDGMENTS

In a book's *Acknowledgments* section, authors frequently recount how long they have been working on their project. At one level, I can't help but bring to my effort the sum total of my living and learning experiences—so I could say in truth "66 years!" But, I would not have cared about this subject at all had my life not been completely transformed by Jesus 45 years ago. However, it has been in the last 10 years that specific research and reflection for this undertaking began in earnest.

In the summer of 2008, Bruce Mandel, a prominent attorney and newly elected Chairman of the Community Relations Committee of the Jewish Federation of Cleveland, Ohio, insisted to his colleagues that he wanted to open a dialogue with evangelicals in the city. Over 30 years ago, Tom Hare began bringing evangelical pastors together to pray which eventually morphed into HarvestNet Ministries and thereby provided an entity with which the Jewish Federation could interact. Without the visionary and courageous leadership of these two men, this book would not have been written.

The HarvestNet Board asked me to be the co-chair along with Rabbi Steven Denker of a Jewish-Evangelical Dialogue group that met quarterly. Later, we added a Pastor-Rabbi Roundtable. I realized early on how ill-equipped I was to co-lead such a group and began asking Rabbi Denker for reading recommendations on Jewish history and rabbinic thought. Thanks, Steve, for your warm embrace and guidance.

This is not the place to try and list all of the wonderful relationships that developed though my contacts with the Federation, but I would be remiss if I did not mention some who had a direct influence on the writing of this book. Special thanks to my Hebrew teacher Rabbi Moshe Adler who, as I wrote in a tribute to him upon his retirement, "taught us about Hebrew and Hebrews." Likewise, I am grateful to Rabbi Moshe Berger for the riches of thought I gained in classes I took from him both at Siegal College and in his home. I'm so appreciative of my rabbinic dialogue partners who ask pointed questions and contributed valuable insights when I shared with our group in outline form some of the core content of what became this book. Last, I want to acknowledge Rabbi Zach Truboff's help in his thoughtful "Jewish Response" to the content I shared and the subsequent books he recommended to me.

To Tom Hare, Steve Erickson, and Rabbi Eric Lakatos for perceptive comments on the manuscript and resource recommendations—thank you dear friends for the gifts of your time and encouragement!

I am also much obliged to the team of good people at HarvestNet Publishing for turning a manuscript into a book.

Most of all, I owe my godly wife Sylvia such a debt of gratitude for her many rereads and corrections of chapters as well as unremitting encouragement, long discussions, and intercessory prayer. I love you, sweetheart!

And, of course, this poor man would have had nothing to write about if the Lord Jesus had not made his salvation known to him on September 16, 1973. Thank you, Lord!

ABOUT THE AUTHOR

Steve Neptune experienced a life-transforming encounter with Jesus Christ in 1973. He has since been engaged in church-planting and equipping leaders in the United States and abroad. He currently serves as the founding pastor of GateWay Church in Aurora, Ohio. Steve is also a founding board member of HarvestNet Ministries, composed of church and marketplace leaders in the Greater Cleveland metropolitan area who share the common purpose of "Engaging God's Vision for the City-wide Church." In this capacity, he carries the responsibilities of serving as president of HarvestNet Institute and as co-chair of the Rabbi-Pastor Roundtable in conjunction with the Jewish Federation of Cleveland. He earned a Master of Christian Ministry degree from the Orlando Institute and a post-graduate studies certificate in The Jewish Background of the New Testament from The Israel Institute of Biblical Studies of Hebrew University in Jerusalem. His first book *The Promise of the Spirit: Why Now?* came out in 2017. Steve and his wife Sylvia have five adult children and eight grandchildren.

Made in the USA
Lexington, KY
23 October 2019